Sunday School
PROGRAMS
for INTERMEDIATES

Sunday School
PROGRAMS
for INTERMEDIATES

Compiled by MARY ALICE BIBY

ASSOCIATE, INTERMEDIATE WORK

Sunday School Department

The Sunday School Board of the Southern Baptist Convention

BROADMAN PRESS
NASHVILLE, TENNESSEE

Copyright, 1946

BROADMAN PRESS

NASHVILLE, TENNESSEE

Second Printing, April, 1947

Printed in United States of America

2.5 AL 477

INTRODUCTION

The purpose of this book is to provide help for the host of volunteer Sunday school workers with Intermediates. These programs were prepared by active Intermediate Sunday school workers and used first by them in their own work and later by others. They, therefore, have come to you out of the actual experience of successful workers in the churches.

The contents of these programs were selected for young people 13-16 years of age. These programs will give Intermediates ideals and ideas out of which they can, and no doubt will, build Christian homes.

The compiler and editor of this book of programs is thoroughly prepared for this task. For many years she has worked successfully with Intermediates and workers with Intermediates in the capacity of associate superintendent of Intermediate Sunday School Work in The Sunday School Board of the Southern Baptist Convention.

These programs can be repeated because promotion of pupils will bring about a complete change of constituency every four years.

Careful selection and adequate preparation of each program will guarantee greater success in performance and results.

J. N. BARNETTE
Secretary of
Sunday School Department
Baptist Sunday School Board

FOREWORD

For many years Intermediate superintendents have wanted a book of complete programs, prepared especially for Intermediate department opening services. I am therefore sincerely grateful to Mary Alice Biby, who has been associated with me in Intermediate Sunday school work since 1925, for compiling this book.

MARY VIRGINIA LEE
Superintendent of Intermediate Work, Sunday School Department, Baptist Sunday School Board

PREFACE

The material for the programs in this book was taken from the *Intermediate Counselor,* a magazine that was published by The Baptist Sunday School Board for more than twenty years.

An effort has been made to preserve the originality of each program. However, changes have of necessity been made in some of them.

To use the programs effectively the primary objective should be to meet the spiritual needs of the pupils. Plan each program so that it will become a contributing factor to the realization of the objective.

Keep the class period in mind as you plan. Coordinate the program and the lesson. If this is done, avoid the use of the lesson passages.

Work for a deep experience of worship including wholesome atmosphere, right attitudes, and heartfelt reverence.

Plan your programs at least three months in advance. Base them upon a close study of your pupils and an equally careful study of the lessons.

Be a persistent collector of materials, such as: songs, stories, poems, pictures, playlets, illustrations, pamphlets, books, and the like. As soon as you have decided on your programs for the quarter, write immediately for pamphlets, pictures, or other materials needed.

See that the assembly room is ready. A clean room is an absolute necessity for good programs. Endeavor to make the room cheerful and attractive. Flowers, greens, a good picture, adequate light, sufficient ventilation, and the entrance at the rear of the room will help.

You will notice that many Scripture passages are used. Endeavor to develop a real love for the Bible. See that passages which you feel are particularly helpful are underscored. Urge that forceful verses be memorized and that an effort is made to put the truths of the Scriptures into daily conduct.

Study each program selected. If you feel that some other song, Scripture passage, special number, poem, or illustration would be more helpful, use it. Be sure, however, that every part is definitely related to the subject selected.

I am grateful to all who have had a part in the production of this book, including copyright owners who so graciously granted permission for the use of material.

MARY ALICE BIBY

CONTENTS

12

DOCTRINAL

REVERENCE TOWARD GOD

Mary Virginia Lee

PRELUDE: "Tread Softly"

CALL TO WORSHIP: "The Lord Is in His Holy Temple"

MEDITATION (led by superintendent): 1. *God is ever-present.*—Is the Lord here? Is God in this room? Open your Bibles to Jeremiah 23:24. (Call on someone to read the reference.) How can this be? I do not know. We do know that a person can speak over the radio and be heard everywhere at once.

When Jacob was fleeing from Esau, he thought he was alone as he slept with his head on a stone; but in a dream he saw a ladder reaching to heaven on which were angels ascending and descending, and he said, "Surely the Lord is in this place; and I knew it not" (Gen. 28:16). He thought he had left God behind.

Open your Bibles to Psalm 139:7-10 and keep this place. (Read as pupils follow.) Could David get away from God? Neither can you or I. Isn't it wonderful that God is everywhere? He can be with us wherever we are and also with our loved ones.

2. *God is all-wise.*—(Call for voluntary responses to the following questions.)

17

How many of you have used a microscope? What is it for?

How many have looked through a telescope? What does it do?

What is X-ray used for?

What does radar do?

All these instruments reveal things that our natural eyes cannot see because they are finite—limited in vision. But God is not limited. He is infinite. He sees not only what we do, but he knows what we think and how we feel. He sees into our very hearts.

Look again at Psalm 139:1-6, 11-12. (Read as all follow.) No one can hide from God. He sees every sinful thought and evil deed.

3. *God is holy.*—When God spoke to Moses from the burning bush, you remember, he told him to remove his sandals because the place whereon he stood was holy.

Let us try to get a truer appreciation of God's holiness as parts of Isaiah's and of John's visions are read—Isaiah 6:1-3; Revelation 4:2-4, 6, 8-11.

4. *Reasons for respect and reverence.*—Why do soldiers and sailors have to salute officers of superior rank? Why do we salute the flag? Why do people stand when the President of the United States enters the room? Out of respect and honor.

What should be our attitude toward such a wonderful God as ours? Should we not be respectful and reverent when we enter his house? When we read his Word? When we speak his name? When we speak to him, should we not kneel or bow our heads and close our eyes and try to realize his presence?

STORY: "Queen Victoria and Handel's *Messiah*"

The closing festivity of Queen Victoria's coronation was the performance of Handel's *Messiah*. . . . When the Hallelujah chorus was being sung, the entire audience, as was the custom, rose to its feet. The court ladies had instructed the young Queen that it would be unbecoming and hardly dignified for her to rise, and that she should, therefore, remain seated, in accordance with royalty's prerogative. But the Queen did not know what mighty emotion was to flow over her soul. There came a few seconds of silence, like the stillness of death, and then the bass, alto, and tenor, in quick succession, sang out the words, "For He shall reign forever and ever." And the sopranos, catching up the song as if inspired, and lifting it almost to the very heavens, proclaimed with their magnificent voices, "King of kings, and Lord of lords." And then together, bass, alto, tenor, and soprano, in one mighty volume of song, rang out, "Hallelujah! Hallelujah! Hallelujah!"

No wonder people rose as Queen Victoria sat there with her crown fresh upon her head, and said, "He is, indeed, King of kings and Lord of lords." Despite the custom of royalty and regardless of what the nation might think, the young Queen rose, folded her hands on

19

her breast, and reverently bowed her head as if she had lifted her own crown from her head and had laid it down before Him.

—Adapted from *Christ and the Fine Arts*, p. 489, by Maus. Published by Harper and Brothers. Used by special permission.

So let us, too, be reverent in his presence.

SONG (all standing, sing third stanza): "Holy, Holy, Holy"

PRAYER

OUR CHRIST

Mrs. John B. Crockett

(NOTE.—Display a large picture of Sallman's *The Son of Man*. Near this picture place an open Bible and a vase of flowers. Darken the room, having only a spotlight thrown on the display.)

CHORUS (sung by a concealed duet): "He Lives on High"

SILENT PRAYER (as concealed duet sings first stanza and chorus of "He Lives on High")

PRAYER VERSE (quoted by one who reads well):

Let the words of my mouth, and the
meditation of my heart, be acceptable
in thy sight, O Lord, my strength, and
my redeemer.—Psalm 19:14

PRESENTATION (led by superintendent): Remember, Christ so loved us that he willingly gave his life for us. May we worship him anew as we consider this blessed truth.

SCRIPTURE READING: "The Incarnate Christ" (Isa. 7:15-16)

DUET (first stanza): "Whispering Hope"

SCRIPTURE READING: "The Vicarious Christ" (John 6:51; 10:11, 15)

SONG (first stanza): "The Lord Is My Shepherd"

SCRIPTURE READING: "The Resurrected Christ" (Matt. 28:1-7)

DUET (first and third stanzas): "Christ Arose"

SCRIPTURE READING: "The Returning Christ"

The words of Jesus (John 14:1-3)

At the scene of the ascension (Acts 1:9-11)

The time of coming not revealed (Mark 13: 32-37)

He is coming in glory and power (Luke 9:26)

SONG (first stanza): "What If It Were Today?"

POEM: "The Risen Christ"

> Beside an open tomb there stands
> The risen Christ with outstretched hands.
> It is yet early, but the dawn
> Is slowly, surely coming on
> With all the light on land and sea
> Gathered in its intensity.
>
> And He who had been sacrificed;
> The living, loving, loyal Christ,
> Who was proclaimed, "I am the Light,"
> A torch set burning high and white,
> Stands in the shadows, cool and dim
> Waiting to draw all men to Him.
>
> The morn may wane, the sun grow pale,
> But His white light will never fail.
> —GRACE NOLL CROWELL, in *The International Journal of Religious Education.* Used by permission of the *Journal.*

SONG (third stanza): "What If It Were Today?"

QUESTION (first stanza and chorus by concealed duet, as all bow heads): "What Will You Do with Jesus?"

PICTURES OF CHRIST

L. N. Stracener

(NOTE.—If possible display copies of the pictures suggested in the following program.)

INSTRUMENTAL DUET (piano and violin): "My Jesus, I Love Thee"

SONG: "Praise Him! Praise Him!"

BIBLE READING FEATURE:

INTRODUCTION (by the superintendent): All of us treasure pictures of our friends and loved ones. In our Bible we have some beautiful pictures of the most precious friend anyone can have—our Saviour. Through the Scriptures and songs we are going to have some of these pictures revealed to us.

SCRIPTURE READING:

1. The birth of Jesus (read by a sixteen-year-old girl): Luke 2:7-14

2. Jesus' baptism (read by a fifteen-year-old girl): Matthew 3:13-17

3. Jesus stills the tempest (read by a fourteen-year-old boy): Matthew 8:23-27

SONG (first stanza): "Peace! Be Still!"

SCRIPTURE READING: Jesus blesses the children (read by a thirteen-year-old girl): Mark 10:13-16

SOLO (first stanza): "That Sweet Story of Old"

SCRIPTURE READING: The transfiguration (read by a sixteen-year-old boy): Luke 9:28-36

23

A SONG PICTURE (sung as a duet): "The Lily of the Valley"

SCRIPTURE READING: "Christ's agony in Gethsemane" (read by a teacher): Luke 22:39-43

A SONG PICTURE (first stanza): "The Old Rugged Cross"

CLOSING COMMENT: (by the superintendent): There is yet a picture of Jesus that no man can paint with sufficient beauty and feeling, either on canvas or in words. It is the picture of the risen Christ who sits yonder at the right hand of God pleading for you and for me to accept him and live for him who died on the cross, giving his life as a ransom for your sins and for my sins. May we keep this picture ever before us!

SONG (first stanza and chorus): "Christ Arose"

STORY (by the superintendent): It is said that a great artist having finished a picture of Christ called in a friend to see it. Long and earnestly the friend gazed upon the inspiring likeness of Christ as painted. Finally, he said, "You have done a magnificent piece of work."

The artist hung his head and said, "Had I known him better, I could have painted him better."

PRAYER: that we may determine to know Christ better

THE HOLY SPIRIT

Homer L. Grice

MEDITATION: "Holy Spirit, Faithful Guide"

SONG: "Holy Spirit, Faithful Guide"

INTRODUCTORY SCRIPTURE READING (by the superintendent, quote from memory):

"God is a Spirit: and they that worship him must worship him in spirit and in truth" (John 4:24).

"As many as are led by the Spirit of God, they are the sons of God" (Rom. 8:14).

"The Comforter, which is the Holy Ghost, . . . shall teach you all things" (John 14:26).

SONG: "Holy Ghost, with Light Divine"

PRAYER: of gratitude for the power of the Holy Spirit in our own lives. Close with:

We pray with the poet,

> Breathe on me, Breath of God,
>   Fill me with life anew,
> That I may love what thou dost love
>   And do what thou wouldst do.
>
> Breathe on me, Breath of God
>   Till I am wholly thine
> Till all this earthly part of me
>   Glows with thy fire divine.
>
> —EDWIN HATCH

DISCUSSION (led by the superintendent): The music, the verses of Scripture that we have quoted, the songs we have sung, as well as the prayer offered, tell that we are thinking together this morning of the Holy Spirit. God is Spirit, and, therefore, invisible to us. "No man hath seen God at any time" (John 1:18). Although we cannot see his face or hear his voice, we can know him, make our wants known to him, and find out what he wants us to do. How can this be? We cannot reveal ourselves to one another except by our bodies. How can God reveal himself to us when he has no body like ours? (Voluntary response.)

Suppose we turn to Hebrews and read the first verse of the first chapter and the first clause of the second verse. (Read in unison.) We cannot see God, but his Son, Jesus Christ, has declared him; that is, revealed him or made him known.

In 2 Corinthians 4:6 we read that Christ commanded "the light to shine out of darkness . . . to give the light of the knowledge of the glory of God in the face of Jesus Christ." God has revealed himself to us—made himself known in the man, Jesus Christ. God, to make himself known to us, became man. What is God like? (Voluntary response.) Yes, he is like Christ; he is the Christlike God. Jesus said to Philip, "He that hath seen me hath seen the Father" (John 14:9).

As long as Jesus was in his body here on the earth, he could make himself known to others; but he was here only thirty-three years. After his resurrection and ascension, he was no longer here in a human body to make himself known to his disciples. If he had not conquered death, he could never have made himself known to us, any more than any other person who dies.

It was because he conquered death that he could and still can make himself known to men. When he was talking with his disciples about his approaching death, he told them that he would not leave them desolate, but would come to them in the spirit of truth and teach them all things that they should know. Let us read these verses together: John 14: 15-18, 22-26; 16:7-14.

The book of Acts and the epistles of the New Testament are all examples of how the Spirit of Jesus, or the Comforter, or the Holy Spirit, made known the will of God to his servants. In the lives of such men as Paul and Peter and John and Stephen, for example, we see the Holy Spirit at work—teaching them, empowering them, guiding them, using them, comforting and encouraging them. Just as the Holy Spirit separated Paul and Barnabas to go out as missionaries to the Gentiles (Acts 13:2), so has he separated missionaries through all the centuries since. Can you name some of them? (Voluntary response.) We read in the New Testament of what Paul could do as a missionary because of the Holy

Spirit; and in men like Livingstone, Carey, Judson, and those of our day we still see what missionaries can do when they are under the leadership of the Holy Spirit.

But it is not enough that only the missionaries and ministers have the Holy Spirit. We, ourselves, also need his presence in our lives. We want him to guide us and teach us. We want really to know God for ourselves, to have fellowship with him, to know when he speaks to us and what he says to us as we face life in all its complexities. God is spirit and we are spirits. His Holy Spirit can and does enter into our lives. What are some things the Holy Spirit has done and will do for us? (Voluntary response.) How may we be sure of his help? (Voluntary response.)

Let us bow our heads and listen attentively and prayerfully while (mention name) reads one of our very finest prayer hymns, "Spirit of God, Descend upon My Heart." (Someone who can really interpret the hymn as a prayer and recite it feelingly should either memorize it thoroughly or become so familiar with the words that to read it will not weaken its effectiveness.)

SOLO (all heads bowed): "Fill Me Now"

PRAYER

GOD THE TRINITY

Mrs. Carl Townsend

ILLUSTRATION: An infidel was scoffing at the doctrine of the Trinity. He turned to a gentleman and said, "Do you believe such nonsense?"

"Tell me how that candle burns," said the other.

"Why, the tallow, the cotton, and the atmospheric air produce light," said the infidel.

"Then they make one light, do they not?"

"Yes."

"Will you tell me how they are three and yet but one light?"

"No, I cannot."

"But you believe it?" The scoffer was put to shame.

—Best Modern Illustrations, Hallock. Used by permission.

CALL TO WORSHIP: "A Mighty Fortress"

SONG: "Holy, Holy, Holy"

SCRIPTURE READING (by pupils): We are going to ask you to quote verses about God. First, we want some verses about God, the Father. (Write "God, the Father" on the blackboard and under it write a few of the most descriptive words from the verses quoted. Some very familiar verses which may be suggested are: Genesis 1:1; Psalm 23:1; Matthew 6:9; John 3:16; Philippians 4:19.)

Now we want some verses about God, the Son. (Write "God, the Son" on the blackboard. Some good verses are: Matthew 1:21; Matthew 20:28; Luke 5:24.)

And the last portion of our Scripture reading is about God, the Holy Spirit. ("God, the Holy Spirit" is written on the blackboard. The following references are good: Matthew 3:16; John 14:16-17; Acts 2:4.)

I am sure there are many questions that arise in your minds on the subject of God the Trinity. We shall try to answer some of them.

(NOTE.—Arrange for a panel consisting of the pastor, Intermediate worker, and Intermediates to sit at the front and develop the program. Urge the asking of questions. However, it will be well to assign a few questions to members of the audience and to have members of the panel prepared to answer them.)

PANEL DISCUSSION:

Question (by member of audience): How do we know that there is a God?

Answer (by a member of the panel): There are many ways to know there is a God. Great students and theologians can name them off to you one right after the other, such as logical proof in the facts of nature and man; comparative religions, creeds, and faiths; the Bible; and finally the revelation in Jesus Christ as proved by history and his influence on history. As we learn about the world and the system of worlds, and as we know ourselves and are honest with our feelings, I feel that it is much easier to be-

30

lieve that there is one supreme Mind and Maker behind it all than to believe that everything simply evolved from nothing.

Question (by a member of the audience): Is there one God or three Gods? How do you explain the Trinity?

Answer (by a member of the panel): Certainly, we believe and the Bible teaches that there is one, and only one God. His name is Jehovah, which means the one who is and shall be. The Bible also teaches, however, that God is manifested in three characters or capacities: God, the Father; the Son; and the Holy Spirit.

Answer (by another member of the panel): As this idea or truth usually seems mysterious and difficult to the human mind, many parallels have been offered. We may find them helpful, although none of them are exact parallels to the great triple personality of God which enables him as Father, Son, or Spirit to meet every need of the human soul.

As water may take the form of liquid, steam, or ice and still be the same chemical elements, so God may assume the form of Father, Son, or Spirit and still be God.

A rose may express itself in color to be seen, or in petels to be felt, or in odor to be smelled. All three expressions are inseparably mixed to make the complete rose. So God may express himself in three

31

ways at different times and places while all three expressions are inseparably mixed to form one complete godhead.

Answer (by a third member of the panel): One of the best explanations I've read was given by Dr. M. E. Dodd at Ridgecrest. He said that at one time he was parent, pastor, and college president to his daughter. At home he was parent to her, at church he was her pastor, and at school her president. Yet, all the time, everywhere he was all three and still just one and the same man. Is that not true of God as Father, Son, and Holy Spirit?

Question (by a member of the audience): I can accept God the Father and God the Son readily as I know them from the Bible and from experience, but I find it difficult to know the Holy Spirit. How can I know and feel him?

Answer (by a member of the panel): I am glad to hear you say "him" in regard to the Holy Spirit for he is a person. He is, of course, God in spirit form. After all, you perhaps know him best, although you may not recognize or realize the fact. He is really the one you know through experience. He convicted you of sin, led you to know God the Father and Jesus as Christ. He is the one who opens the truth of the Scriptures to your heart.

SONG: "Holy Spirit, Faithful Guide"

PRAYER

ASSURANCE OF THE RESURRECTION

Mary Virginia Lee

PIANO SOLO: "Face to Face"

MEDITATION (first stanza): "Speak to My Heart"

DISCUSSION: "The Evidences of the Resurrection"

INTRODUCTION (by superintendent): Cursed is he who would rob one of his belief in the resurrection; for therein lies man's only hope. Nothing can take its place. When hope is destroyed, only despair is left. No hope, no happiness. In the face of death, nothing brings greater consolation than confidence in the resurrection. Let us consider some evidences.

1. *As Seen in Nature* (by a teacher): Spring with its bursting buds, flowering plants, and awakening life is a testimony of the resurrection. All seeds which, when planted, die and produce new plants are evidences. Everywhere nature is reminding one of life after death.

Lord Lindsay's party, while wandering among the Egyptian pyramids, found a mummy which, from the hieroglyphical inscriptions found in the sarcophagus containing the body, was supposed to be 3,000 years old. After unwrapping the mummy, a small root was found in one of its hands. Desiring to know how long vegetable seed-life could exist, the bulb was taken from that hand, closed for 3,000 years, and planted in a sunny soil.

In time it sprouted, blooming into a beautiful flower.

—Copied from *625 New Bible Stories and Illustrations*. Used by permission of the publisher, George W. Noble, Chicago, Illinois.

2. *As Seen in Belief in Immortality* (by a teacher): In the soul of every human being there has been planted a hope of life beyond the grave. As the American Indians believed in the "Happy Hunting Grounds," so evidences have been found among every people of belief in immortality. (Read 1 Cor. 15:51-57.)

3. *As Seen in Prophecies* (by the song leader): Looking forward to the coming Messiah, prophets of the Old Testament speak. (Read of David in Psalm 17:15; of Hosea in Hosea 13:14; of Moses in Mark 12:26-27.)

4. *As Seen in the Empty Tomb* (by the pianist): Mark 16:1-6

5. *As Seen in Appearances After the Resurrection* (by the superintendent): Furthermore, Jesus showed himself alive after many infallible proofs as recorded by different men at different times and different places.

(1) To Mary Magdalene in the garden, Sunday morning, the day of his resurrection (Mark 16:9).

(2) To the other women in the morning of the same day (Matt. 28:9).

(3) To the two disciples on the way to Emmaus, Sunday afternoon (Luke 24:13-35).

(4) To all the apostles except Thomas that Sunday night (Luke 24:36-43).

(5) To all the apostles, with Thomas, the next Sunday night in Jerusalem (John 20:26-31).

(6) To seven apostles by the Sea of Galilee (John 21:1-12).

(7) To five hundred disciples (1 Cor. 15:6).

(8) To James, the brother of Jesus (1 Cor. 15:7).

(9) To the eleven apostles (Matt. 28:16-20).

Two irreligious young men were discussing the resurrection, telling each other why it was impossible for them to accept the doctrine. Then Deacon Myers came passing by, and in a joking way one of the young fellows called to him: "Say, Deacon, tell us why you believe that Jesus arose again!"

"Well," he replied, "one reason is that I was talking with him for half an hour this very morning." We all may have experimental proof of his resurrection and presence.

—*5000 Best Modern Illustrations*, Hallock. Used by permission.

TESTIMONIES (urge all to participate): "What the Assurance of the Resurrection Means to Me."

SONG: "Face to Face"

PRAYER

RESURRECTION DAY

Mrs. Lee MacDonell

(NOTE.—Place a bowl of lilies at the front of the room.)

CHORUS (concealed voices): "He Lives on High"

SONG (first and fourth stanzas): "He Whispers His Love to Me"

SCRIPTURE READING (quoted by the department): John 3:16

PRAYER: of thanksgiving to God for our Saviour

SOLO (first stanza): "One Day!"

SCRIPTURE READING (by superintendent): Luke 2:8-12

SCRIPTURE READING (by the department): Isaiah 9:6

SOLO (second stanza): "One Day!"

CHORUS (first stanza by boys): "The Old Rugged Cross"

SCRIPTURE READING (by the girls): John 19:38-42

SOLO (third stanza): "One Day!"

SCRIPTURE READING (by superintendent): John 20:1

SOLO (by a girl dressed in costume of Palestine): "In the Garden"

SOLO (fourth stanza): "One Day!"

SCRIPTURE READING (by the teachers): John 20: 19-22

36

DOCTRINAL

SONG (first stanza by the department): "Christ Arose"

SOLO (fifth stanza and chorus): "One Day!"

SCRIPTURE READING (by the superintendent): Matthew 13:33, 36-37

(NOTE.—The song "One Day!" may be found in the *Modern Hymnal* or *Songs of Faith*. If you cannot secure a copy of it, you may have someone who reads well to read each stanza as it is called for in the program outline.)

ONE DAY!

One day when heaven was filled with his praises,
  One day when sin was black as could be
Jesus came forth to be born of a virgin—
  Dwelt amongst men, my example is he!

One day they led him up Calvary's mountain,
  One day they nailed him to die on the tree;
Suffering anguish, despised and rejected:
  Bearing our sins, my Redeemer is he!

One day they left him alone in the garden,
  One day he rested, from suffering free;
Angels came down o'er his tomb to keep vigil;
  Hope of the hopeless, my Saviour is he!

One day the grave could conceal him no longer,
  One day the stone rolled away from the door;
Then he arose, over death he had conquered;
  Now is ascended, my Lord evermore!

One day the trumpet will sound for his coming,
  One day the skies with his glories will shine;
Wonderful day, my beloved ones bringing;
  Glorious Saviour, this Jesus is mine!

Chorus

Living, he loved me; dying, he saved me;
  Buried, he carried my sins for away;
Rising, he justified freely forever:
  One day he's coming—O glorious day!

—Used by permission of The Rodeheaver-Hall-Mack Company.

FINAL APPEAL (by the superintendent): Some of you perhaps are not ready for his coming. Will you not seek diligently the way of salvation and give your hearts to him on this glorious morning?

PRAYER

HEAVEN A PLACE

Mrs. W. C. Boone

(Note.—Place a large open Bible at the front of the room. Arrange to have different pupils read the references from this Bible as called for. Ask that all mark the references in their own Bibles as read.)

Instrumental Duet (violin and piano): "When We All Get to Heaven"

Song (first stanza): "Sweet By and By"

Story (by the superintendent): A Christian man, whose little boy, an only child, died, had been living as many Christians do. He had turned away from God, rarely went to church, never attended prayer meeting, and had given up his Bible reading entirely. The night after the little boy was buried, his wife saw him get his Bible and read a long time, stopping every now and then to mark some verses. Night after night he kept this up. The wife wondered what he meant but was afraid to ask him, fearing that it might cause him to give up his Bible reading.

Finally her curiosity got the best of her and one morning she got his Bible, turned the leaves and found that he had marked only the verses mentioning heaven. Then it was plain to her. While the little boy was with him, he cared little about heaven; it was all vague and misty and indefinite, but now that the idol of his heart had been taken from him, the grief-stricken father was trying to

39

learn all he could about the place to which his little boy had gone.

Now I am sure some of you, because of the death of a loved one, have become vitally interested in heaven. Often heaven doesn't become a definite place to us until God comes and breaks the heartstrings and takes our loved ones away .

BIBLE STUDY (led by the superintendent): Let us do just what that father in the story did—take our Bibles and find out what we can about the place called heaven. One hundred years from now all of us will be in heaven or hell. The choice lies with each of us. If you have accepted Christ as your personal Saviour, you have your name written in the Lamb's book of life. Heaven will be your home.

There is a great deal of speculation among Christians as to *where* heaven is and *what* it is like. We really know very little about heaven; yet, there are some things we can know.

Heaven is a place for the redeemed: Matthew 6: 20; John 14:1-3. You cannot lay up treasures unless there is a place where you can lay them up. Jesus said, "I go to prepare a place for you." Then heaven is a *place,* as definite a place as your hometown. What that place is matters not. "Many mansions" means a large and more beautiful place than we can describe. Let us open our Bibles to Revelation 21:17-21 and read it in unison.

Now, let us think of several plain statements that are made in God's Word concerning conditions as they will be in heaven.

1. Heaven is full of joy and happiness and usefulness (Matt. 25:20-23). One of the joys of heaven will be perfect knowledge. The why of everything will be made clear.

2. Heaven shall have "no night" (Rev. 21:23-25). The horrors of night! God does not like darkness. "Men loved darkness rather than light, because their deeds were evil." It is in the night under cover of darkness that most crimes are committed. The evildoer loves the night when nobody can see his wickedness, but God sees at all times! At least half of our time is spent in darkness. Let us use the daylight hours for God—telling others of his love and about the home that he has gone to prepare.

SOLO: "No Night There"

PRAYER: that the unsaved in the department will realize their lost condition

BIBLE STUDY (continued by the superintendent):

3. Heaven shall have no pain, no sorrow, no death (Rev. 21:4). Many of you boys and girls may not have had any sorrow, suffering, pain, and death, but look around and you will see it on every hand. Isn't it a blessed promise that God shall wipe away all tears in that beautiful home, and we shall mourn no

41

more? There will be no more death, no more suffering, no more pain. How glorious!

4. Heaven is a place where we will be with God (John 14:2-4; Rev. 21:3). The greatest promise Jesus gave us about heaven is that we are to be with him there—"so shall we ever be with the Lord." Yes, we will know our loved ones in heaven, too. With our perfect knowledge each of us can say, "I shall know even as I am known" is certainly true. But I rather think we shall spend most of our time looking on Jesus in his beauty and his glory and his wonderful light.

DISCUSSION: Heaven, a place—who shall enter? (John 5:24.) Oh, to know that you are going to heaven when you die! Jesus not only told us something about heaven, but he told us *how* to get there. There's only *one* way—just one means of entrance—"Ye must be born again." How can you be born again? That is why Jesus came (John 3:16).

CLOSING APPEAL

PRAYER

(This program is adapted from the book, *Heaven, Hell and Other Sermons*, by T. T. Martin.)

THE PRINCE OF THE POWER OF THE AIR

Mary Virginia Lee

PRELUDE: "Faith Is the Victory"

SONG: "My Soul, Be on Thy Guard"

STORY: "The Prince of the Power of the Air"

Say, have you ever thought what a fight you could put up if you were invisible? Why, you could walk right up in front of a fellow and smash his nose or knock him down before he could put up his guard or smash back— and even then he couldn't see you to hit you. Of course, that would be a cowardly thing to do, but I'm just saying "Suppose." And this is to introduce right here your arch enemy, the devil, who is not a "suppose" at all, but is very real, very personal, and very invisible,—always present and ready to do his cowardly, dirty work.

Somebody said people are like a lot of safes. We may be generally of the same pattern, but each has a different combination. Perhaps none of us knows the combination to any but our own, but the devil carries them all in his notebook, and he never makes the mistake of trying to throw a fellow with a drink when his combination is a cigarette, or vice versa.

The devil's finger is in all our affairs, and we can keep nothing secret from him. No matter what we try to do, he is ever present to try to make us do it his way. Even when we worship God, or pray, or sing, he has the audacity to try to make suggestions. You think the Wright brothers were clever to "conquer the air," and they were; but the devil has won the title of "Prince of the Power

43

of the Air"! His airplane is instantaneous and noiseless;
he requires no special landing field, but he can light on
the lobe of your ear with a precision that is uncanny,
and, lighting there, he whispers things into your heart
that you would not dare utter with your lips. There are
three points scored on the Wrights in one breath, and
there are many others.

The devil has won victories over the best men we can
think of. Oh, how he got David, and spoiled a wonderful record being made by the "man after God's own
heart." All in a trice he tripped David and led him to
break six of the Ten Commandments at once—five to ten
inclusive! And he got Moses for a bad fall, and Elijah
and Abraham and Jacob. He simply crept up unseen
and caught them with their guards down.

But in spite of the fact that he took a fall out of each
of those strong and saintly characters, he met his match
and more than his match when he tackled our Saviour.
He made the strongest attack that could have been made,
but Jesus overthrew him and put him to flight, and today's big news is that there is a way for you and me to
throw this fellow down. Simple enough, if you are on
your guard. Did you notice how Jesus handled him?
He quoted Scripture to him. Scripture to the devil is
just like salt on a snail. He can't stand it.

Jesus used God's Word, and that is invincible even
against the devil, our mightiest foe. Go into your Bible
and select an assortment of "devil-chasers." Memorize
them and have them ready for instant use. Like David,
choose five smooth stones from the "Brook" and put
them in your scrip; then you will be ready for this giant,
who stalks abroad as a roaring lion seeking whom he

44

may devour. Only, he doesn't roar: he is noiseless and invisible—don't forget that.

—*Say, Fellows!* by Wade C. Smith. Used by permission of Fleming H. Revell Company.

We cannot withstand Satan in our own strength. He is "the prince of the powers of darkness." When Peter felt so sure that he would not forsake Jesus, you remember, that very night he denied Christ. Paul knew of the trickery of this prince quite well, too; therefore, he warns us and urges us to be prepared.

SCRIPTURE READING: Ephesians 6:11-14

SONG (first and second stanzas): "I Need Thee Every Hour"

PRAYER: (Close with chorus of song sung very softly while heads are bowed and eyes are closed.)

THE REALITY OF HELL

Mrs. W. C. Boone

SOFT MUSIC: "Throw Out the Life-Line"

CHORUS: "Throw Out the Life-Line"

PRAYER: that hell may be made so real to us to-day that each will turn from his sinful ways and follow the Master

SCRIPTURE READING (read by two boys and two girls): Psalm 9:17; Mark 9:43-48; John 3:36; Revelation 22:11

DISCUSSION (led by the superintendent): As you have listened to these Scripture passages, I am sure you have been impressed that hell is real. It has become fashionable in these days not to believe in the reality of hell. Many people who possess the highest education (so called) are in the position of the drunken man who staggered on the stage while the late lamented infidel, Robert G. Ingersoll, was delivering one of his witty orations, attacking the fundamentals of Scripture teaching. The intoxicated man dodged the watchman at the stagedoor and before he could be stopped, he was on the stage with the distinguished lecturer. "Mr. Ingersoll," he interrupted, "are you sure there is no hell?"

"Yes, I am sure of it and I can prove it," answered the famous infidel.

"Well, I'm glad to hear you say that," returned the tramp, "because that's what folks like you and me will have to depend upon." And sad to say there are many today, infidels and agnostics, who are depending upon a belief that there is no hell as their only hope of escape, when we have just read from God's Word, "The wicked shall be turned into hell, and all the nations that forget God."

Thus we have seen that this Book tells of a place called hell. Don't delude yourself and don't let the serpent or his allies deceive you into believing that it is not so. It is not pleasant; the thought is horrible, but so is cancer or tuberculosis horrible. Nevertheless, both are dreadful realities.

DISCUSSION (continued by the superintendent): Many facts about hell are clearly revealed in God's Word. (Assign the following Scripture references to pupils before the program begins. The superintendent may comment on each as he sees fit.)

1. In hell you will never be free from sin (Psalm 57:3).

2. In hell you will be useless for all eternity ("chaff" means eternal uselessness) (Psalm 1:4).

3. In hell there is remorse, gnawing at the soul as the years come and go (Luke 13:28).

4. In hell sinful nature, thirst, and suffering are ungratified (Luke 16:23-24).

47

5. In hell associations are horrible. What crowd do you choose? (Rev. 21:8; 22:15.) Everyone who rejects Jesus will be in that crowd.

6. In hell you remember (Luke 16:25). Your sins pass before you.

7. In hell there is eternal separation from the redeemed and from the Lord (Matt. 7:23).

Is there a real hell for sinners? See what Jesus said: Matthew 25:41-45 (read by the department). How can hell be avoided? There is a way of escape. Just one!

CHORUS: "One Door and Only One"

CLOSING WORD (by the superintendent): That's why Jesus came—to make it possible for us to escape hell. It is either hell or "Believe on the Lord Jesus Christ, and thou shalt be saved" (Acts 16:31).

SOLO: "Where Will You Spend Eternity?"

FINAL APPEAL (by the superintendent): Call for all who are lost and wish to escape hell and to be remembered in prayer to raise their hands.

PRAYER (as pianist plays softly, "Where Will You Spend Eternity?")

(This program is adapted from the book, *Heaven, Hell, and Other Sermons*, by T. T. Martin.)

A MEMORIAL (Baptism)

Mrs. Elbert F. Hardin

VIOLIN SOLO: "Abide with Me"

PRAYER SONG: "Open My Eyes, That I May See"

DISCUSSION (led by the superintendent): What is the most interesting memorial you have seen? (Voluntary response.) You know almost as soon as America entered World War II we began to see service flags in homes, offices, shops, factories, schools, hospitals, and churches. Many of our churches have bought handsome plaques and displayed names of men and boys who served their country. There were many gold stars placed upon those flags and plaques as memorials to men who gave their lives. When men died at sea, or overseas, their bodies were not brought home, and so memorial services were held for them.

The greatest leader of all ages, Jesus Christ, went out of the world and left orders for his soldiers to keep marching until victory over evil was won forever. He went from our view, but he remains in close contact and he still directs all battles; we may be confident of victory if we follow his leadership.

Before he left the world in his bodily form, he commanded his followers to do two things to perpetuate his memory, and so we hold these memorial

49

services in order that we may honor his teachings and remember his love and sacrifice.

What is the first of these memorials? (Voluntary response.) Yes, baptism. Each person observes this when he joins the church. Let us read together the account of Jesus' baptism. Matthew 3:13-17.

Jesus set us the example. Then, when he was going back to heaven, he left us a command about it. Again let us read Matthew 28:19-20.

Baptists believe five very important things about baptism. (Have pupils read all Scripture references.)

1. Will you look at your open hand? Suppose we name the little finger "command," for Jesus *commanded* baptism as we have just read. Peter urged it (Acts 2:38) and the apostles practiced and taught it. We believe we must keep such a command, example, and teaching if we obey the Bible.

2. We shall call the next finger "immersion," for the *act* of baptism is *immersion*. The boys will please read Mark 1:9-10; the girls, John 3:23. Now all of us will read Acts 8:38-39. What do these verses prove? Yes, that baptism means immersion.

3. The longest finger shall be named "salvation," the most important thing in the whole world. Salvation precedes baptism. Only those who repent of their sins and believe in Christ as their personal

Saviour should be baptized. The Great Commission which we read says "make disciples" before it says "baptize." Many Scripture references give us grounds for this belief. Acts 2:41; Mark 1:4-5; Acts 16:33-34.

4. Our fourth finger has an odd name, "administer," for only an authorized baptized believer should *administer* baptism. The act was performed by the authority of Christ. John the Baptist was a preacher commissioned by God to baptize those who repented of sin. The apostles practiced the act. We infer from the New Testament teachings that baptism is a church ordinance and the pastor is the regularly authorized person to baptize other believers into the church.

5. We shall call the thumb "symbol," for baptism is a picture or symbol. It pictures our death to sin and our resurrection to new life. It is also an outward profession of our faith in Christ. Romans 6: 1-4. Now can you name and explain these five important things about baptism? (Have a hand drawn on the blackboard. As pupils name each of the five in order, write each one as given on the proper finger.)

Later we shall study the other memorial, the Lord's Supper.

APPEAL (by the superintendent): Now that you have realized the importance of baptism and its spiritual foundation, will not you who have accepted Christ as your Saviour but have not joined the church do so and be baptized? Won't you run over the five things named on your fingers and decide not to put off baptism any longer? And you who are not saved, won't you believe in Christ this morning? Won't you accept him as your Saviour? Then will not you, too, join the church and follow Christ's example in baptism?

SOLO: "Why Not Now?" (Ask that all heads be bowed as the chorus is sung the last time.)

THE SUPPER OF OUR LORD

Mrs. Joe Trussell

(NOTE.—Display a picture of the Lord's Supper. Darken the room and throw a spotlight on this.)

CHORUS (by concealed voices): "I Love Him"

DUET: "My Jesus, I Love Thee"

SONG: "I Love Him"

SENTENCE PRAYERS (by four class presidents): that we may love and appreciate Jesus more and live closer to him

DISCUSSION (led by the superintendent): Every circumstance of life must have a time, a place, and a person or persons present. This morning let us make this application to the Lord's Supper. First, let us see at what *place* this Memorial Supper was instituted. Who can find and read Mark 14:12-16?

Now, who can tell us the *time* of its institution? (Voluntary response. Answer: the evening before the crucifixion of our Lord.) Who were the *persons* present when the Supper was actually partaken of? (Voluntary response.) Let us read together Mark 14:17-18 and Luke 22:19-20.

For what purpose did Jesus establish the Lord's Supper? (Voluntary response. Answer: "This do in remembrance of me.") If, then, this Supper is

53

the Lord's, he alone shall decide *who* is to partake of it, and *when* and *where* it is to be partaken of.

SONG: "Break Thou the Bread of Life"

(NOTE.—Write in large letters on the blackboard the three words, one under the other: Who? When? Where?)

DISCUSSION (continued by the superintendent): It would be an unpardonable breach of etiquette if you were to invite yourself to dinner at the table of the President of the United States. He names his guests and sends out invitations himself. To *whom,* then, does Jesus give the invitation to eat at the Lord's table? (Await response and encourage it. Answer: Only baptized believers.) Who are baptized believers? (Bring out the fact that Baptists believe that immersion of a *saved person* is baptism. Therefore, sprinkling or pouring is not baptism and will not qualify one to partake of this Supper in a Baptist church. Emphasize the fact that with Baptists only the immersion of one who has already been saved is baptism. Make it clear that a person, to be scripturally baptized, must *first* have believed on Christ and been saved by him, and then immersed.)

(NOTE.—Opposite the word "Who" on the blackboard, write "Baptized believers.")

DISCUSSION (continued by the superintendent): Now *when* shall this supper be observed? Can you think of any place in God's Word which tells us how often we should partake of the Lord's Supper? (Vol-

54

untary response.) "For as often as ye eat this bread, and drink this cup, ye do shew the Lord's death till he come" (1 Cor. 11:26). Since we are not told how often, do you think it should be observed every Sunday as is the practice of some denominations? (No, because it would soon lose its significance.)

(NOTE.—On the blackboard opposite the word "When" write "This do ye, as oft as ye drink it, in remembrance of me.")

DISCUSSION (continued by the superintendent): Our last question is: *Where* should this Memorial Supper be observed? Should it be carried into the homes? Let us read Paul's admonition to the Corinthians concerning this. 1 Corinthians 11:20, 22, 34.

A family had gathered for its annual reunion in the farm home of one of its members. As one of the brothers was a minister and all were church members, the suggestion was made that they take the Lord's Supper, which they did in the family living room. Was this right? Why not? (Because it is a church ordinance and should be observed in the church.) The Lord's Supper is not a "communion" between brothers and sisters but between baptized Christians and the Lord. He said, "This do in remembrance of me."

(NOTE.—On the blackboard opposite the word "Where" write "In church.")

CONCLUSION (led by the superintendent): Let us all read together from the blackboard the questions and answers which have been written there. Following this we will stand and sing with bowed heads the first stanza of "I Gave My Life for Thee."

PRAYER

EVANGELISTIC

WINNING TO CHRIST

Mary Alice Biby

(NOTE.—Display a large picture of Christ and also a number of books on soul-winning. It would help to have a number of evangelistic Bible verses in conspicuous places.)

SOFT MUSIC: "Why Not Now?"

SONG (first stanza): "Softly and Tenderly"

SCRIPTURE READING (unannounced, read by a concealed reader): Ezekiel 33:7-9

INTRODUCTION (by the superintendent): It is said that 400,000 boys and girls are passing from the Intermediate departments of the South each year without Christ; that means that, on the basis of past achievements, 340,000 or 85 per cent of these will never be saved. (Place these figures on the blackboard.) God deals with each soul in strict justice. He would have each unsaved one turn from his wicked way and serve him. Let us see, according to God's Word, what the penalty is for one who does not accept him.

SCRIPTURE READING (reread by the department): Ezekiel 33:7-9

DISCUSSION (by the superintendent): Have you a lost friend in danger of paying this penalty? What is the penalty of the Christian who has an opportunity to win a soul to Christ and yet fails to do so? (Read a third time Ezekiel 33:8 and ask each pupil to underscore this verse in his Bible.) Can another discharge your responsibility as a soul-winner? Why? (Voluntary response.) What should be the motive in winning souls to Christ? (Voluntary response.) Let us study some requisites to soul-winning as found in God's Word. (Give the following references to pupils to read.)

> Be saved—Isaiah 45:22
>
> Love Christ—Matthew 22:37
>
> Love souls—Romans 10:1
>
> Be prayerful—James 5:16
>
> Know God's Word—2 Timothy 2:15
>
> Be clean—Psalm 51:10
>
> Be uncompromising—Ephesians 5:15
>
> Be tactful—2 Corinthians 6:3-4a
>
> Be guided by the Holy Spirit—Psalm 31:3

(NOTE.—If possible, have a copy of the references for each member of the department. Perhaps the chairman of activities will make them. Try to make each suggestion personal. Ask each person to check himself on these requisites.)

DISCUSSION (led by the superintendent): How may we make opportunities for soul-winning? How may we make the approach in leading a soul to Christ? How may we use God's Word? (Give opportunity for voluntary response to each of these questions.) Begin with the individual where he is. If he realizes that he stands lost and condemned in God's sight, then begin with repentance. If he is repentant of his sins, then begin by showing him he must believe. The one with whom you are dealing must realize that he:

Is a sinner.   Isaiah 53:6

Is condemned.   John 3:18

Must repent.   Luke 13:3

Must believe.   John 3:16

The saved should realize that he:

Must confess Christ.   Matthew 10:32-33

Must obey Christ.   John 14:15

Should be baptized.   Romans 6:4

Should partake of the Lord's Supper.
1 Corinthians 11:23-26

Should serve.   Hebrews 12:28;
Romans 12:1

(NOTE.—The above references may be assigned to classes or to individuals to read when called for.)

QUESTION (asked by a teacher): What things other than personal work may we do in soul-winning? (Voluntary response.) Urge prayer lists and prayer groups.

SILENT PRAYER: (After a moment of silent prayer, the leader may quote the following.)

Look on the harvest field so white
Soon comes the darkness of the night;
Go, in the name of Jesus go,
Every Intermediate ought to know.

—Adapted from "Every Sunday School Ought to Grow," McKinney

MEDITATION (directed by the superintendent): I am wondering, in the silence of this quiet time while all heads are bowed, if each of you who are saved will not think of one lost person whom you would like to win to Christ? Now may we have some sentence prayers asking for divine leadership as we covenant with God that we will try to lead at least one soul to him?

SENTENCE PRAYERS

PRAYER CHORUS: Following the prayers, while all remain with bowed heads, ask the entire department to join in singing the chorus, "Lead Me to Some Soul Today."

BEING A CHRISTIAN

Mary Virginia Lee

PRELUDE (played very softly): "Moment by Moment"

SOLO: "There's a Great Day Coming"

PRAYER

DISCUSSION (led by the superintendent): "What It Means to Be a Christian"

We speak of people being Christians. What is a Christian? What does it mean to be a Christian? Here on the blackboard are two figures representing a boy before he was a Christian and after he became a Christian. He was a fine-looking boy, neat in his appearance, kind, courteous, and intelligent before he was a Christian, just as he is now. Then what is the difference? Let us find out from God's Word.

(On the blackboard draw the figures and write the outline given below.)

BEING A CHRISTIAN

Before	Scripture
Dead	Ephesians 2:1
Sinner	Romans 3:23
Blind	Ephesians 4:18
Condemned	John 3:18*b*, 36*b*
Child of devil	John 8:44
Headed for hell	Psalm 9:17

After	*Scripture*
Alive	John 5:24
Seeing	1 Timothy 1:15
Not condemned	John 9:25
Saved	John 3:16, 18a, 36a;
Child of God	Romans 8:1
Home in heaven	1 John 5:1 and 2 Corinthians 5:17
	John 14:2

ON WHICH SIDE ARE U?

DISCUSSION (by the superintendent): "How to Be a Christian"

1. A lost person must realize that he *needs* to be saved:

He is a *sinner*—Romans 3:23

He is *condemned*—John 3:18; Romans 6:23; Mark 9:48

Only one who can save—Acts 4:12

No escape if salvation is neglected—Hebrews 2:3

Now is the time—2 Corinthians 6:2; Proverbs 27:1

2. He must accept God's plan:

Repent—Luke 13:3

Believe—Acts 16:31

STORY (by the superintendent): "Changed Lives"

One day, it is related, Queen Victoria visited a papermill. The owner showed her through the works, not

64

knowing who she was, and among other places took her into the rag-room. When she saw the filthy, dirty rags, she exclaimed, "How can these ever be made white!"

"Ah, lady," was the reply, "I have a chemical process of great power by which I can take the color out of even those red rags." Before she left he discovered that she was the Queen.

A few days after, the Queen found lying upon her writing desk a lot of the most beautifully polished paper she had ever seen. On each sheet were the letters of her own name and her likeness. There was also a note which read as follows: "Will the Queen be pleased to accept a specimen of my paper, with the assurance that every sheet was manufactured out of dirty rags which she saw on the backs of the poor rag-pickers, and I trust the result is such as even the Queen may admire. Will the Queen also allow me to say that I have had many a good sermon preached to me in my mill? I can understand how the Lord Jesus can take the poor heathen, and the vilest of the vile, and make them clean, and how though their sins be as scarlet, he can make them white as snow. And I can see how he can put his own name upon them; and just as these rags transformed may go into a Royal Palace and be admired, so poor sinners can be received into the palace of the great King."

—1300 Quests and Conquests, p. 244

DUET: "Though Your Sins Be as Scarlet"

TESTIMONY AND APPEAL

SONG: "Softly and Tenderly"

GOD'S WAY OF SALVATION

Mrs. John Hathaway

(NOTE.—Arrange for the one taking the part of God's Word to stand in the balcony [if there is one] or in the rear of the assembly room where he can be heard well, but not seen. His voice should be full and clear and he should be a good reader. The superintendent may ask the question and the reader should give all Scripture references in full.)

SOFT MUSIC: "I Know the Bible Is True"

INSTRUMENTAL DUET: "The Way of the Cross Leads Home"

PRAYER: that the Holy Spirit may help us to understand God's way of salvation

COMMENTS (by the superintendent): There are many who differ on the plan of salvation. Some say the way to be saved is to live a good moral life; others say the way to be saved is to be baptized; still others think that the giving of alms to the poor will save the soul. We are not going to take any of these as authoritative, but this morning we are going to let God's Word speak to us on the way of salvation. We can be sure that what God says in his Word is true, so I am going to ask some questions. Let us listen closely while the Word of God speaks.

QUESTION: Word of God, what provision has been made for our salvation?

WORD OF GOD: "Christ Jesus came into the world to save sinners" (1 Tim. 1:15).

QUESTION: Who are sinners?

66

WORD OF GOD: "All have sinned, and come short of the glory of God" (Rom. 3:23).

QUESTION: If all have sinned and are lost, what did Jesus do to take away our sins?

WORD OF GOD: "Christ died for our sins according to the scriptures" (1 Cor. 15:3).

QUESTION: Was that the reason Jesus had to hang on the cruel cross and suffer?

WORD OF GOD: Isaiah 53:5-6

DUET (first and third stanzas): "I Gave My Life for Thee"

QUESTION: But what have we to do in order that our sins may be laid on Jesus?

WORD OF GOD: Isaiah 55:7

QUESTION: If any of our boys and girls who are lost would forsake their way and turn to Jesus this morning, would he receive them?

WORD OF GOD: "Him that cometh to me I will in no wise cast out" (John 6:37).

QUESTION: But how may they really know how to come?

WORD OF GOD (Read each of the following): Luke 13:3; John 3:16; Romans 10:9-10

QUESTION: Does that mean all who are here this morning who have not accepted Jesus as their Saviour?

WORD OF GOD: "Whosoever will, let him take the water of life freely" (Rev. 22:17). "As many as received him, to them gave he power to become the sons of God, even to them that believe on his name" (John 1:12).

QUESTION: Is there no other way to be saved except through Jesus?

WORD OF GOD: (read the following): John 14:6; Acts 4:12

QUESTION: This last question: Is there not plenty of time for the lost to give their hearts to Jesus?

WORD OF GOD: Isaiah 55:6; also, "Behold, now is the accepted time; behold, now is the day of salvation" (2 Cor. 6:2).

MUSIC (played softly as superintendent tells story): "Let Jesus Come into Your Heart"

STORY (by the superintendent): God's Word has spoken to us very plainly. It has told us that all are lost without Jesus; that there is only one way to be saved, and that way is Jesus; that to receive him one must forsake his own way and come believing him with his heart and confessing him. Are you lost this morning?

A boy was once lost in the woods of Maine. For hours he wandered about seeking a way out, but each way he turned he found himself in a denser part of the woods. Suddenly he realized that he was completely lost, and sank to the ground in deepest despair. He was cold, hungry, and frightened. He had heard that the forest was infested with wild animals. In a trembling voice he began to call loudly, "Lost! Lost!"

A dog's bark answered. Then a man's voice said, "Stay where you are, and I will come and get you." He waited anxiously. In a few minutes he saw between the trunks of the trees the light of a lantern. A man said in a quiet voice, "Follow me." The boy followed. In his soul was the joy of the feeling, "I am saved! I am saved! I am saved!" What a feeling it was! Such a feeling comes to all who, lost in sin, behold the Light of the world and heed without hesitation the voice of the Lamb of God, when he saith, "Follow me."—*The Intermediate Quarterly*

If you are lost this morning, Jesus can save you and save you now. Let every Christian bow his head in prayer. (Ask soloist to sing softly two stanzas of the song, "Let Jesus Come into Your Heart.") Ask all who will trust Jesus as their Saviour to raise their hands.

PRAYER

REPENTANCE

Ethel Hudson Williams

VIOLIN SOLO: "I Need Jesus"

SONG: "Let Jesus Come into Your Heart"

PRAYER: that God, through his Holy Spirit, may teach each one the meaning of repentance

SPECIAL MUSIC (piano and violin accompaniment): "I Heard the Voice of Jesus Say" (Found in *Songs of Faith.*)

(NOTE.—Place the following outline on the blackboard. Write all Scripture references shown in the outline on slips of paper and give to pupils before the program begins. Assign the subjects to be discussed to teachers at least a week in advance.)

SALVATION

Jesus the author and giver of salvation

Man's Part	*God's Part*
Repent: Romans 2:4	Forgive: 1 John 1:9
Believe: John 1:12	Regenerate: John 3:7; 1:12-13
Confess: Romans 10:9-10	
Forsake: Acts 26:20	Justify: Romans 5:18
	Adopt: Romans 8:16-18

Repentance the key to eternal salvation

Matthew 9:10-13

DISCUSSION (led by the superintendent): "Man's Part"

Repentance shows us God's mercy, his long-suffering, and his love toward us in giving us a new chance, not only for this life, but for eternal life with him.

70

The word "repentance" in the New Testament comes from a Greek word, *metan' oy ah* meaning a change of mind. It is a change of mind regarding sin. It is seeing sin as God sees it. It is sorrow for sin. Not sorrow that sin has found us out, but sorrow that we have offended the holiness of God. (Read 2 Cor. 7:10.) In other words, it properly denotes an afterthought, or the soul recollecting its own actings, and that, in such a manner, as to produce sorrow and a total change of heart and life as we see from the outline on the blackboard. Repentance produces a conviction of sin, confession of sin, and a hatred of sin, which causes one to forsake it. (Call for Scripture references which are listed on the blackboard under "Man's Part.")

Repentance is the key that unlocks the door to eternal life with God. It is conviction or a knowledge of sin, contrition or sorrow for sin, and conversion or turning from sin and to Jesus Christ. (Read Matthew 9:10-13 and give your own comments on these verses.)

TELEGRAM (brought in by a messenger boy and read by the superintendent): "I tell you, Nay: but, except ye repent, ye shall all likewise perish" (Luke 13:3).

QUESTION (discussed by a teacher): Who is the author of salvation? Christ, God's Son, is the author. He gave himself to make it possible for everyone who would repent and accept him to be saved. Repentance turns us from the way of sin and death into the way of life and truth. God is the finisher of our salvation. He has the final part. Then the result of repentance brings pardon, peace, and eternal life as God forgives, regenerates, justifies, and adopts us as his children. Repentance brings to each of us the very best blessings. Let us think about these blessings.

DISCUSSION: "God's Part"

(NOTE.—Call for Scripture references [to be read by the department] listed on the blackboard under "God's Part." Make necessary comments as follows as each reference is given. Teachers may take these parts if preferred.)

1. Forgiveness comes from two Greek words. One means "to send away" and emphasizes the act of forgiveness. The other means "to freely give," the manner of the act of God in bestowing favor on sinful man. Forgiveness is based on the death of Christ. The death of Christ does two things: reveals the infinite love of God and his infinite power over sin. Forgiveness (God's act) follows repentance (man's act).

2. Regeneration is necessary for all because of the sinful nature of man. Jesus said, "Ye must be born again" (John 3:7). Regeneration means a new nature given by Christ.

DUET OR QUARTET (department joins in on the chorus of the last stanza): "Ye Must Be Born Again"

72

3. Justification means a new standing before God. It is God's judicial act in which he declares the *repentant* sinner free from guilt and restored in divine favor. God is just and holy. Man is sinful. God cannot compromise his justice. Therefore, the death of Christ does two things: it takes away our sins and preserves the justice of God. Justification comes only when a sinner turns from sin by *repentance*.

4. Adoption means a change of family—a new relationship to God. Repentance of sin and the acceptance of Christ makes us a child of God—the greatest blessing that can ever come to anyone.

Hence, we see how repentance is the key that opens to us eternal life and a blessed happy life here on earth; and remember, "Except ye repent ye shall all likewise perish." If you are lost, what are you going to do about it? Will you think this matter through and turn to God? Will you accept Jesus Christ as your Saviour through repentance and faith?

SONG: "Just As I Am"

PRAYER

BELIEVE ON THE LORD JESUS CHRIST

Mrs. E. A. Patterson

MEDITATION (by pianist and violin): "Tread Softly"

CHORUS: "Only Believe"

QUESTION (by the superintendent): Today we want to discuss the subject, "Believe." There is a vast difference in believing about certain things and believing in them. How many of you brought your Bible this morning? Please hold them up so that we may see them. Is there a difference in believing that there is a Bible and believing in the Bible? (Voluntary response.)

SCRIPTURE READING (read by boys): Acts 16: 23-31

SONG (first stanza and chorus): "I Know the Bible Is True"

DISCUSSION (led by the superintendent): In our Scripture reading we find a man who is an officer of the law at Philippi, ready to take his own life. He hears the voice of one whom he thinks has escaped. Paul's voice stays the hand that would take life. After seeing that all the prisoners are there, he realizes that some miracle has been wrought. I think his fear of the man turns to fear of God. Will you read the question again that he asks Paul and Silas,

74

"Sirs, what must I do to be saved?" What is Paul's answer? "Believe on the Lord Jesus Christ." We do not need an earthquake to make us see that we are lost. We need just to open our Bible.

SCRIPTURE READING (read by the department): John 3:18; Mark 16:16

DISCUSSION (continued by the superintendent): We have God's Word to tell us just what unbelief on Christ means and what the penalty is. To put it in terms of the business world—what salary does it pay? (Eternal death.) What does believing on the Lord Jesus Christ pay? (Eternal life.)

Believing on the Lord Jesus Christ involves more than just saying we believe. It must come from the heart and must not only involve belief but must go further and trust Christ.

STORY (by the superintendent):

One must not only believe that Jesus Christ is the Son of God, that he died and made atonement for the sins of men, but he must also *trust* Christ with his own personal salvation.

Suppose that a man has a thousand dollars and goes into a bank with it.

"I have a thousand dollars in my pocket," he says to the cashier, "and I want to put it where it will be safe. Is this bank all right? Would my money be safe here? And could I get it whenever I want it?"

"Yes, this bank is a safe place for your money," declares the cashier.

"Well," says the man, "I am afraid of banks. I have heard of people who lost money in them. You will have to prove to me that this one is safe."

"All right," says the cashier, "let me show you about everything here and explain to you how we take care of money."

"Everything surely looks all right," says the man after he has been shown through the bank. "I do *believe* that my money would be safe here."

If he walks out with the thousand dollars still in his pocket, has he exercised faith in the bank? No, he has not.

If, however, after examining everything he makes out a deposit slip and hands in his money to the cashier and goes out leaving it there, he has exercised faith in that bank. He not only *believed* that the bank could take care of his money, but he also *trusted* it to take care of it. That is faith—belief and trust.

For one to have faith in Christ, he must *believe* that Christ is able to save him and he must actually *trust* Christ to save him. The man left his money in the bank. The bank is now responsible for the safekeeping of that money. The man himself now has no responsibility in the matter. So one must trust his soul's eternal salvation entirely into the hands of Jesus Christ! "Trusting Jesus, that is all!" That is what Paul did, for he said: "I know whom I have believed, and am persuaded that he is able to keep that which I have committed unto him against that day" (2 Tim. 1:12).

—*The Plan of Salvation*, pages 79-81, Dr. Austin Crouch. Used by permission.

SCRIPTURE READING (read by the teachers and officers): Romans 10:9

CONCLUSION (led by the superintendent): God is here this morning. He has promised that where people gather in his name he will be in their midst. In the quietness he speaks to us telling us to believe on the Lord Jesus Christ for salvation—to put our trust in him. Will you let him speak to you?

SOLO: "Why Not Now?"

SOFT MUSIC: "Only Believe"

PRAYER

WHAT WILL YOU DO WITH JESUS?

Mrs. W. J. Bolt

(Note.—Write on the blackboard, "What will you do with Jesus?")

Soft Music: "Almost Persuaded"

Solo (first and second stanzas): "What Will You Do with Jesus?"

Introduction (by the superintendent): This is the one question I want to ask each unsaved pupil this morning. It is found in Matthew 27:22. "What shall I do then with Jesus?" Will you bow your heads as our soloist repeats ever so softly the chorus, "What Will You Do with Jesus?" (Soloist sings.) Unsaved one, will you take this question seriously and think it through as she sings? This question has faced each one of us and it has either been answered or must be answered sooner or later. What shall *I* do with Jesus? There are different ways of disposing of Jesus and we want to study about some of these today. Several of our boys and girls will tell us what some have done with Jesus.

Rejected him.   Matthew 19:22; 11:20-23

Delayed accepting him.   Acts 17:32; 24:25

Opposed him.   Luke 22:63-66; 23:1-5

Sought him.   Acts 8:30-31; John 3:1-7

Accepted him.   Matthew 4:18-20; Acts 2:41

SOLO (third stanza): "What Will You Do with Jesus?"

DUET (concealed in back of room or classroom—unannounced): "Almost Persuaded"

DISCUSSION (led by the superintendent): We have seen what disposition some people have made of Jesus and their example should either be a warning or an encouragement to you. Can you not accept him now? He is anxious to save you but you must want to be saved. Jesus never forces himself on any heart. He will only come in at your invitation. Won't you open the door of your heart and let him in? He is standing at your heart's door right now seeking admittance. What will you do with him today?

Have you ever seen the lovely picture of Jesus standing at a closed door knocking? (Show the picture, "Light of the World," by Hunt.) A friend of the artist asked him if he had not forgotten something. He asked what. The friend said the door had no knob.

"Well, that is as I intended," said the artist. "The door must be opened from the inside."

There is no outside doorknob of the heart; it has to be opened from within. Are you willing to open the door of your heart? Jesus is there waiting now.

SOLO (unannounced): "Let Him In"

REQUEST (by the superintendent): Will all Christians sing the last stanza as heads are bowed, and will all unsaved who will invite Jesus into their hearts hold up their hands?

PRAYER

MITS OF THE BIBLE

Mrs. Eureka Whitaker

(NOTE.—Have "Saved" and "Unsaved" printed on the blackboard in large letters.)

SOFT MUSIC: "Softly and Tenderly"

PIANO DUET: "The Way of the Cross Leads Home"

SCRIPTURE READING (read in unison): Romans 10

WORD STUDY (led by the superintendent)

INTRODUCTION: There are just two classes of people in the sight of God. I wonder who can tell me what they are? Yes, they are saved and unsaved. Were these two classes born saved and unsaved? (Voluntary response.) No, the saved were not born saved. When they became old enough to know right and wrong, they had to take certain steps to be saved. We are going to think about "mits" of the Bible. Four pupils are going to tell us some things one must do to be saved.

(NOTE.—Have four mits cut out of white cloth and sewed up so they may be slipped on the hand. On the front side of one print "AD"; on another, "SUB"; another, "COM"; and on the last, "TRANS." Give the following parts to four pupils and have each hold up the hand with the mit on it as he speaks.)

1. "Admit." The unsaved must admit that they are lost. (Read Rom. 3:23 and Psalm 32:5.) The saved must admit that they haven't done their best. (Read Luke 9:59-62.)

SONG (second stanza): "Give of Your Best to the Master"

2. "Submit." The saved must submit to whatever operations are necessary to bring them to God. This must be done through repentance and faith. (Read James 4:7-8.)

3. "Commit." The saved need to commit their ways and plans more completely to the Lord. (Read Psalm 37:5.)

4. "Transmit." (Read Matt. 28:19-20.) Even though the Great Commission had not been given, we should want the saving power of Jesus transmitted to others because of gratitude. How can we help in this?

STORY (by the superintendent): When we utilize these "mits," we can do more for Jesus. Our faith is increased in our Lord and our ability strengthened.

One day, almost three hundred years ago, a schoolmaster asked his favorite pupil, "Don't you think, John, that the time has come to recognize the claims of Jesus Christ?"

The lad, John Eliot, was touched by the earnest words, gave himself to the Master, and some years later became the "Apostle to the American Indians." Half a century after his death a young man, David Brainerd, very sorrowfully, fearing that God would not use him, was handed by his friend, Jonathan Edwards, a copy of the *Life of John Eliot.* After reading it, he said, "I will take up John Eliot's work where he left it."

For two years he wrought nobly among the Indians; then God called him home. But his influence did not end. A poor cobbler in England, William Carey, read the *Life and Letters of David Brainerd,* became oppressed with the darkness of the heathen world, and interested his neighbors; began to preach, and was instrumental in the founding of the modern missionary movement; and was sent to India by the Baptist Missionary Society as their first missionary.

—Sunday School Journal

Will you follow the example of these great men? Will you use these "mits"?

PRAYER

THE DANGER OF DELAY

Joe Trussell

(NOTE.—Place red flags [may be made of red paper] about the department, at the entrance, in halls, and on stairways leading to the department. If assignments are made, place these on red flags. Secure several danger signals and arrange in conspicuous places. As each danger signal in the program is given, place a danger signal at the front with poster carrying the key word of the Scripture.)

CHORUS: "There's a Great Day Coming"

DISCUSSION (led by the superintendent): Have you ever, while making a journey, come upon a red flag waving before you? Of what was it a signal? (Voluntary response.) What would you expect if you deliberately ran over this signal of danger? (Voluntary response. Destruction.) God has placed along the journey of life red flags warning us of danger ahead.

1. One of the first danger signals is the danger of hardening our hearts against Christ. Every time we reject Christ, our hearts grow harder. God tells us in Proverbs 29:1 what will happen to those who continue to harden their hearts. Will someone read this please? That is danger signal number one.

2. The next danger signal is that of putting off salvation to some future time, although we have no assurance of a single tomorrow. Let us read Luke 12:16-21 together. God did not call this man foolish because he was rich or because he grew a great crop and wanted to build a barn to take care of it.

84

Why was he foolish? (Voluntary response. Because God says *now* is the time of salvation and the man trusted in the future.) Boys and girls, do not make the mistake this man made, but heed the voice of God when he says, in Isaiah 55:6, "Seek ye the Lord while he may be found, call upon him while he is near." God will not always strive with those who continue to reject him.

SOLO (first and second stanzas): "Why Do You Wait?"

DISCUSSION (continued by the superintendent): Again, we find that it is dangerous to delay because it is the devil's cleverest method of luring souls to hell. The devil would say, "Have a good time while you are young. Dissipate. Waste your talents and forget about your soul. When you are old, there will be time enough to think about salvation."

But what does God's Word say? Will someone read Ecclesiastes 12:1? The devil used this method of destroying the soul of Felix when he caused him to say in Acts 24:25, "Go thy way for this time; when I have a more convenient season, I will call for thee." But we have no record that the "convenient season" ever arrived or that Felix ever called for Paul to tell the apostle that he had accepted Christ. Procrastination is not only the thief of time, but it is the thief of souls.

SONG (first stanza): "Almost Persuaded"

DISCUSSION (continued by the superintendent):

3. The third danger signal is the warning that death is certain and often sudden. Perhaps you have read or heard of the tragedy of the New London School at New London, Texas, where boys and girls, many of them of your age, were quietly studying when suddenly an explosion occurred which hurled over five hundred of them into eternity to meet God without any warning or time for preparation. Some of them may have delayed the important matter of their soul's salvation. Perhaps they thought they had ample time, but death is certain and often sudden.

SOLO (third and fourth stanzas): "Why Do You Wait?"

DISCUSSION (continued by the superintendent): Do you dare delay this important decision? Your soul will spend eternity in one of two places, heaven or hell. One day Jesus will say to those on his left hand, "Depart from me, . . . into everlasting fire" (Matt. 25:41), and to those on his right hand, "Come ye blessed of my Father, inherit the kingdom prepared for you from the foundation of the world" (Matt. 25:34). (Draw a vertical line on the blackboard. Place Matt. 25:41 on the left side and Matt. 25:34 on the right side.) Upon which side will you be? *Now* is the time to heed the danger signals. *Now* is the time to determine where your soul will spend eternity. "Behold, now is the accepted time; behold, now is the day of salvation" (2 Cor. 6:2). Do not delay. Accept him *now*.

PRAYER: for the unsaved of the department

INVITATION SONG (If led by the Holy Spirit, make a further plea for acceptance of Christ): "I Am Resolved"

CHURCH MEMBERSHIP

NEW OBLIGATIONS

(Church Membership)

Chester L. Quarles

PRELUDE: "Work, for the Night Is Coming"

SONG: "To the Work"

DEFINITION: Define "church membership."

SCRIPTURE READING (read by the department): Psalm 116:12-14

PRAYER

DISCUSSION (led by the superintendent): What kind of a person should a church member be? What are the responsibilities and obligations of a church member?

(NOTE.—Open discussion. The pupils will suggest various things but the superintendent will be able to sum them up as follows: (1) attendance upon the services of the church; (2) stewardship; (3) soul-winning; (4) doctrinal stamina; (5) missionary studies and activities, and participation in all the church work.)

QUESTION (by the superintendent): What do we mean by saying the church member ought to attend the services of the church?

ANSWER (by a boy): A member of any kind of organization ought to be loyal to its meetings. When we realize how important the church is to us all our lives, we realize how important it is to attend the services. First, we ought to attend the services because of what they mean to our lives. The only way to learn to worship is to worship. One can only learn to pray by praying. We need to attend because of the encouragement it will give others who may or may not be Christians. Certainly our pastor is happy when church members express their loyalty and support by coming to the preaching services, the prayer services, and the teaching and training services.

QUESTION (by the superintendent): That is true. What do we mean by saying the church member should be a good steward?

ANSWER (by a girl): A steward is a trustee. Every church member should realize that he is a trustee of his time, his talents, his money. He is God's agent and should seek to render a good accounting for God. One is responsible not only for paying the tithe, but for rightly using the nine tenths. Also he is responsible to God for the proper use of time and talents.

DUET: "Trust, Try, and Prove Me"

QUESTION (by the superintendent): Yes, we should be good stewards. What about soul-winning?

ANSWER (by a boy): The Bible says, "He that winneth souls is wise." The desire to win another to Christ ought to be the first impulse of a new Christian. All of Jesus' life and teachings cause us to know that he considered it most important. His call to his followers was a soul-winning call. The Sermon on the Mount is evangelistic through and through. His contacts with individuals, his parables, and his sending out of the seventy focus attention upon his passion for souls. Jesus is our example. It is our privilege to seek to win souls. This includes the worldwide missionary task. (Read Matt. 28:19-20.)

QUARTET: "Wherever He Leads I'll Go"

QUESTION (by the superintendent): Is it desirable for a person to be a loyal and staunch member of his church?

ANSWER (by a girl): Yes; a member of a Baptist church ought to be proud of the fact. He should endeavor to know the fundamental and distinctive doctrines of Baptists. We believe that the Baptist doctrine should be studied. Someone has said, "Give a person an open mind and an open Book and he will be a Baptist."

QUESTION (by the superintendent): What is the greatest tragedy of many churches?

ANSWER (by a girl): The fact that there are so many unenlisted church members in Baptist churches. This is a major calamity. It is estimated that 65 per cent of Southern Baptists are unenlisted. This means that a great host of Baptists are not giving their money to the Lord's work, are not attending services in his church, are not winning souls, or teaching Sunday school classes. In fact, their Christian life seems static. Every Christian ought to be a participating member, taking an active part in the full life of the church.

BLACKBOARD CONCLUSION (by the superintendent): Suppose we plan to practice some of the things suggested, or things not suggested, in which we have been negligent. If you, in the quietness of this hour, have decided on some definite obligation as a church member which you have determined to assume, will you please mention it? (List on blackboard.)

PRAYER (by an adult): that God will help us to discharge our personal obligations as church members

MY CHURCH

John Farmer

(NOTE.—Let the program be in the form of a discussion. Arrange for several to sit in a circle at the front of the room, and take the different parts. If songs are sung, ask the department to join in the singing of "My Church." A cardboard church is suggested for use in portraying the privileges of church membership.)

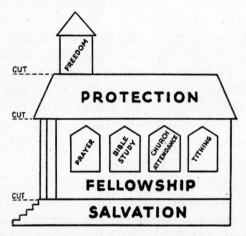

Direction for making pasteboard church. Draw and cut out a large picture of a church. Then cut it into four sections as shown by the dotted lines on the drawing. The main body or wall of the church may represent "Fellowship"; the roof, "Protection"; the steeple, "Freedom"; and the foundation and front steps, "Salvation." Cut four windows out of cardboard and paste yellow cellophane across the back of them. The windows will represent "Enlightenment"—Prayer, Bible Study, Church Attendance, and Tithing. Print "My Church" across the top of a large piece of poster board and fasten it on the wall at the front of assembly room. As the talks are made, the speakers will place their part of the church building on the poster board.)

SOFT MUSIC: "My Jesus, I Love Thee"

1. *Fellowship.*—I am glad that I am a church member. I love my church. Why, I get to associate with the best people. You know, I feel that I need to associate with the best so that I can be the best Christian possible. I want the influence and examples of Christians to guide and help me, and this I get in my church. The fellowship of Christians warms my heart and leaves its imprint on my daily life. (Read 1 John 1:3 and then pin the walls of the church on the poster.)

2. *Protection.*—To me my church is a place of shelter in time of storm. (All listen as concealed soloist sings the chorus of "The Haven of Rest.") Yes, that's just it. I'm safe for truly my church is a fortress when oppressed; a refuge against rebuffs; and a camp which criticism cannot break up. Doubt and fear may come upon each of us and oppression may come in the form of ridicule and slander, but in the church of the Lord Jesus Christ we have a bulwark of safety. God's love overshadows his church like the roof over our heads. (Place roof on the church and then read Matthew 18:20.)

3. *Enlightenment.*—(Pin the four windows on the church while speaking.) The church is a great light

shining into the deep of God's riches, showing us happiness, joy, and peace. If we would be enlightened and understand God's plan for us, we must open the window of *Prayer;* put in the light of *Bible Study;* follow the beam of *Church Attendance;* and let the joy light shine because of our *Tithe.* (Read Psalm 18:28.)

SONG: "Sweet Hour of Prayer"

4. *Freedom.*—How we thrill as we think of freedom! Our church rings out the glad tidings of freedom of conscience, freedom of worship, freedom of church government. Our Saviour died for his church, and freed us from the bondage of sin, liberated us from the clutches of Satan. I think we ought to ring out the good news to all the world. (Pin the steeple on the church.)

SONG (fourth stanza): "America"

5. *Salvation.* (Pin the steps and foundation on the church.) And now we shall add the foundation —salvation through Jesus Christ. This is the most important part of it, because we must have salvation—that is, be born again—to enter into Christ's church. (Pianist plays softly, "Where He Leads Me.") Are you saved? Have you been born again? Have you trusted Jesus completely and wholly for your salvation? Will you give him your heart and your life? What does it take? Repentance toward God, and faith toward our Lord Jesus Christ. As

many as received him, to them gave he power to become the sons of God, even to them that believe on his name. Do you believe? (Soft music: "Why Not Now?") Will you confess him publicly by raising your hand while we sing softly?

SONG: "Have Thine Own Way, Lord"

CLOSING THOUGHT (by the superintendent): I trust each of you who are church members will endeavor to put more into your church membership, and that you who have been saved but have not become church members will do so at once. Then, how I do yearn for the unsaved to accept Christ and become active church members.

PRAYER

CHRISTIAN LIVING

LETTERS

Mrs. J. W. Marshall

PRELUDE: "Living for Jesus"

SONG: "More Like the Master"

INTRODUCTION (by the superintendent): It was the custom even hundreds of years ago for the Jewish brethren to bring letters of recommendation with them from their churches. And then, even as now, those letters were sometimes misused. It is a rather serious thing to write a letter of recommendation. Does it not look suspicious for a man to carry about with him a lot of letters of recommendation, for those letters do not make the man. One man has said, "Whenever you see a chimney with a big log up against it, you may know it is a weak chimney and needs to be propped." The purpose of a letter of recommendation is to give a person an introduction—then it is up to that person to live up to that recommendation and prove his worth.

SCRIPTURE READING (Before reading, explain that in this passage Paul is speaking of letters of recommendation.): 2 Corinthians 3:1-4. Paul is saying, "I do not need a letter of recommendation, because you and your changed Christian lives are my recommendations. You are a letter of Christ which I have been employed to inscribe." A letter carries a message to someone from someone. This message was from God and it was sent to the sinful people of the world. But what was the message that this epistle brought? It was the message of salvation and everlasting life. And Paul said that the message was so important that it was not written with ink, nor even on tables of stone—God wrote this message on the "fleshy tables of the heart."

DISCUSSION (led by the superintendent): "Letters"

But do you suppose that these Christians in Corinth were the only letters which carried Christ's message to the world? No, indeed! Every time a soul is born into the kingdom of God that soul is Christ's letter to the world. Every time a man becomes a Christian that man has a message from God to the lost and dying world. You and I, then, if we have accepted Christ as our personal Saviour, have a message from God to present to the sinful world. I wonder if we are worthy epistles? Can God's message be read in our lives? Let us look at our epistles, our messages.

First Letter: (Secure six large white envelopes and on them print in the upper left-hand corner: From God, the Heavenly Father; address the envelope: To the Sinful People [first line]. In the World [second line]. Holding up envelope.) This envelope represents our lives which carry a message from God. On it we read: To the Sinful People in the World. What is the first thing you want to do when you receive a letter? (Voluntary response.) All right, then, let us open this envelope and look into our own hearts and find the message God has written there. (Open the first letter which is only a blank piece of paper.) Isn't it always a thrill to get a letter and open it? (Holds up letter.) Can you read this message? What is wrong with it? (Voluntary response—nothing written on it.) I wonder if we live so faraway from God and talk to him in prayer so seldom that we have lost the message for salvation that he has given to the world. There are people dying for a message from God— they are depending on us to give it to them. If we do not have a message from God, then we should pray, pray, and pray until God speaks that message and writes it in our hearts, so all of the lost people can read it and come to know him.

Second Letter: (Open the second letter and hold it up. On this have John 3:16 written very dimly with a pencil.) Can you read this message that God has for the world? (Voluntary response—too dim.) I wonder if the message on our hearts is that dim—because we fail to pray, because we fail to read the Bible, because we fail to come to God's house to worship, and because we are crowding out God's will in our lives. Stop and think before you go farther—God is holding you accountable for giving the message of salvation to the world.

Third Letter: (Open the third letter. On it is written John 3:16, but the ink is badly blurred.) Can anyone read this letter? (Voluntary response —too blurred.) Is the message God has given you so blurred that the world cannot read it? Have you compromised with the world? Are you just giving God a part of the tithe? Are you just giving him a part of your life?

Fourth Letter: (Open the fourth letter. On it is written the same message, but it is almost completely covered with small advertisements of worldly things, clipped from newspapers.) Surely, we will be able to read this message? No! It is covered up with sinful habits and worldly amusements. It has been said, "The things you do speak so loud I cannot hear what you say." God cannot use you to carry his message to the lost world as long as you live with the world. Is the world worth the price? It makes you pay and pay and pay. Unless we give up worldly things we will never know the greatest joy in the world—the joy that comes from doing God's will.

Fifth Letter: (Open the fifth letter. On it is written the same message but holes are burnt in the paper and it is so soiled that the message cannot be read.) Can you read this message? (Pause for voluntary response—too soiled.) There are too many little sins covering the message. They are not big sins, but they hide God's words. Smutty stories, bad words, evil deeds have covered up the message of God. If you would be God's messenger, your life must be dedicated "a living sacrifice" to him.

Sixth Letter: (Open the sixth letter. On this John 3:16 is written in clear letters so that everyone can read it.) Can you read God's message in this letter? (Holds it up. Ask all who can see it to read it together.) "For God so loved the world, that he gave his only begotten Son, that whosoever believeth in him should not perish, but have everlasting life." That is the message of salvation—the words of life. That is the message God would give to the world through you. There is not a more powerful sermon in the world than a consistent Christian life. Christians' lives are the only religious books or letters many people will ever read. God has written this message to the lost and dying world—we are the King's epistles, signed with his blood on Calvary. Are you living so the world can read this message? I hope each person present will determine from now on to so live that lost people can read God's message in your life, and that you will surrender your life to Christ and become a messenger for him.

Are you willing to live for Jesus? To give him your all? To dedicate your life to him? If you are, please raise your hand during the song.

SOLO: "I Surrender All"

PRAYER: of dedication

MAKE EACH DAY THE MASTER'S

Mary Alice Biby

TELEGRAM (read by the superintendent): "I really want to make each day the Master's. Will you please tell me how?—An Intermediate."

SOLO: "O Master, Let Me Walk with Thee"

MEDITATION (led by the superintendent): "How to Make Each Day the Master's"

I wonder if the yearning as shown in this telegram and solo is not one that is often in the heart of each of us. How may we make each day the Master's? How may we live in and for and through him? Shall we bow our heads in silent prayer as we get further help on how to make each day the Master's?

SOLO (first and last stanzas, unannounced and sung softly, though loud enough to be heard by all): "Sweet Hour of Prayer"

SCRIPTURE READING: Philippians 4:6 (prayer); Hebrews 4:16 (come boldly); 1 Thessalonians 5:17 (pray unceasingly)

QUESTION (by the superintendent): Would it not be well to form the habit of speaking no word on awakening each morning until a word has first been spoken to the Master?

A moment in the morning, ere the cares of day begin;

107

Ere the heart's wide door is open for the world
to enter in,
Ah, then alone with Jesus, in the silence of the
morn
In heavenly sweet communion, let your duty
day be born.
In the quietude that blesses with a prelude of
repose
Let your soul be smoothed and softened, as the
dew revives the rose.
                                    —ARTHUR LEWIS TUBBS

Surely the first step in living for Jesus is to *want*
to live for him. The second step is to spend much
time in *prayer* as we seek directions on how to live
for Jesus.

TESTIMONIES: Suppose several of you tell how
prayer has helped you in your effort to make each
day the Master's. (It may be well to notify several
previously so that this period will not lag.)

FLASH CARDS (shown by pupils and read as
shown, then thumbtacked to the wall so all may see
them): I think these flash cards will further emphasize how to live for Jesus.

> Be conscious of and practice God's presence.
> Exercise a greater degree of patience.
> Be more thoughtful of others.
> Show more love for others.
> Cultivate strength to resist temptation.
> Observe a daily devotional.
> Do something for others each day.

QUESTION (by the superintendent): What else is necessary in order to make each day the Master's?

SCRIPTURE READING (read by the department): Psalm 119:11 (God's Word). In God's Word each of you can find not only the secret for making each day the Master's but inspiration as well as courage and strength to live each day for Jesus.

CHORUS: "Thy Word Have I Hid in My Heart"

SCRIPTURE READING: Acts 17:11 (search the Scriptures daily)

> A moment in the morning, take your Bible in your hand,
> And catch a glimpse of glory from the peaceful promised land;
> It will linger still before you when you see the busy mart,
> And like flowers of hope, will blossom into beauty in your heart,
> The precious words, like jewels, will glisten all the day,
> With a rare effulgent glory that will brighten all the way.
> When come a sore temptation, and your feet are near a snare,
> You may count them like a rosary and make each one a prayer."
>
> —SELECTED

OPEN DISCUSSION: "When and How to Read God's Word to Gain Help in Making Each Day the Master's"

SHORT TALK: on service based on John 9:4

DUET: "It Pays to Serve Jesus"

REQUEST (by the superintendent): I have given each of you a slip of paper. Will you please write at least two things you are going to do in your effort to make each day the Master's?

PRAYER

PRAY BELIEVING

Lucile Hawkins

(NOTE.—Arrange a telephone on the table at the front of the department.)

DUET OR QUARTET: "What a Friend"

SILENT PRAYER

SOLO: "Sweet Hour of Prayer"

QUESTION (asked by an Intermediate and addressed to the superintendent): What is prayer?

ANSWER (by the superintendent): Prayer is the soul's sincere communion with God. It is talking to God and letting him talk to you.

DISCUSSION (led by the superintendent seated at the telephone): As I sit down to the telephone, I am in touch with thousands of individual wires over which messages are transmitted to all parts of the country. You can pick up your telephone in your home and talk to a loved one or a friend in New York or out on the Pacific Coast some three thousand miles away. But before you call that person, you must *believe* that he is at the other end of the line and that he will hear and answer you.

If you do not believe that, you will not call. This brings us to the first point in our discussion this morning. There is but one line leading to the throne

of grace; one line between you and God. That line
is belief.

(NOTE.—Give out the following Scriptures on Bibles cut from catalogues
and pasted on paper.)

SCRIPTURE READING (introduced by the superintendent): We have some messages direct from God
this morning. They are translations as found in
God's great Book of messages and they tell us how
to talk with God more effectively. Several of you
will give these, adding your own comments.

1. When ye pray, believe . . . that God is. (Heb.
   11:6)

2. When ye pray, believe . . . that God is near.
   (James 4:8)

3. When ye pray, believe . . . that God hears you.
   (1 John 5:14-15)

4. When ye pray, believe . . . that the Holy Spirit
   helps you. (Rom. 8:26; Gal. 4:6)

5. When ye pray, believe that Christ intercedes
   for you. (Rom. 8:34; Heb. 7:25)

DISCUSSION (continued by the superintendent):
Now that we have heard some of the essentials of
effectual prayer, let us think again about our telephone lines.

Did you ever call someone over the phone and
have "Central" say, "There is something wrong on
your line; hang up and dial again, please"?

Did you ever get someone over the phone and have that person at the other end of the line say, "Something must be wrong; I cannot hear you, you sound so faraway"?

Did you ever call "long distance" and hear the operator on the line helping you get your message through?

Did you ever try to get someone on the phone after a storm, and find that there was no connection —that the line had been severed?

The trouble on the telephone line may not be your fault because telephones are man-made, but when there is trouble on the line that leads to the throne of grace that is your fault. It isn't God's. God's ear is ever listening, listening for the slightest audible sound of your heart. I'm wondering if you are hindering God from hearing and answering your prayers. There are so many hindrances. Suppose we list some of these on the blackboard. (Voluntary response.) Stress the following:

1. Are you *living so faraway from God* in your Christian life that he cannot hear you?

2. Are you *ignoring the Holy Spirit*, whom God sent into the world to help you, and who wants to help you—who will help you if you will let him?

3. Are you *ever conscious that Christ is always interceding* for you?

4. Have you let *the storms of fear and doubt sever the line* until there is no contact with God?

5. Are you *afraid to trust God,* to take him at his word, to step out on his promises?

You are to pray without doubting. Doubt is an insult to God; it is mockery; it is questioning his love, his goodness, his promises, his ability to answer prayer.

A little doubt can spoil all your faith. God says, "Whosoever shall say . . . and shall not doubt in his heart, . . . he shall have whatsoever he saith" (Mark 11:23). "Therefore I say unto you, What things soever ye desire, when ye pray, believe that ye receive them, and ye shall have them" (Mark 11:24).

If there is anything wrong on that individual line of yours leading to God, will you not repair that line? Will you not begin this morning?

TESTIMONY (by a consecrated man or woman): "What Keeping Open the Individual Line Between God and Me Has Meant to Me"

PRAYER

USE THE BIBLE EFFECTIVELY

Bonnie Thomas

(NOTE.—On a table at the center of the front of the assembly room place a large copy of the Bible with a bowl of flowers near. Arrange other copies in different languages, translations, and versions about the room.)

SOFT MUSIC: "Holy Bible, Book Divine"

SONG: "Wonderful Words of Life"

PRAYER: that God's Book may mean more to each one present

HOW DO YOU READ (led by the superintendent, placing the following on the blackboard):

Wrong Way	*Right Way*
Thoughtlessly	Purposefully (under-
Toilsomely	standing)
Occasionally	Reverently
Carelessly	Prayerfully
	Regularly

TESTIMONIES: "My Most Helpful Bible Verse and How It Has Helped Me"

QUOTATION (by a boy):

The Bible is one of the greatest blessings bestowed by God on the children of men.—It has God for its author; salvation for its end, and truth without mixture for its matter.—It is all pure, all sincere; nothing too much; nothing wanting.

—LOCKE

DISCUSSION (led by the superintendent): "How to Get Help from My Bible for Effective Christian Living"

John Ruskin has said, "Make it the first morning business of your life to understand some part of the Bible clearly, and make it your business to obey it in all that you do understand."

Some of you are going to help me by reading references as we think of some reasons for studying the Bible. (Place the following reasons on the blackboard as given.)

> For the way of salvation—Luke 13:3; John 3:16
>
> For inspiration—Isaiah 40:31
>
> For security—Isaiah 41:10, 13
>
> For guidance—Proverbs 3:1-6
>
> For obedience—John 14:15
>
> For service—Romans 12:1
>
> For rest—Matthew 11:28-30
>
> For comfort—John 14:1-3

QUESTION: What are some good habits to form in studying the Bible? (Voluntary response.) The following suggestions may be brought out:

> Go to the Bible for help with every life problem.
>
> Read the Bible daily.

Make notes of helpful thoughts received. Review these often.

Put into practice what you read in the Bible.

Hunger for knowledge from God's Word.

POEM: "When I Read the Bible Through"

I supposed I knew my Bible,
    Reading piecemeal, hit or miss,
Now a bit of John or Matthew,
    Now a snatch of Genesis,
Certain chapters of Isaiah,
    Certain Psalms (the twenty-third),
Twelfth of Romans, First of Proverbs—
    Yes, I thought I knew the Word!
But I found that thorough reading
    Was a different thing to do,
And the way was unfamiliar
    When I read the Bible through.

Oh, the massive, mighty volume!
    Oh, the treasures manifold!
Oh, the beauty and the wisdom
    And the grace it proved to hold!
As the story of the Hebrews
    Swept in majesty along,
As it leaped in waves prophetic,
    As it burst to sacred song,
As it gleamed with Christly omens,
    The Old Testament was new,
Strong with cumulative power,
    When I read the Bible through.

117

Ah, imperial Jeremiah,
  With his keen, coruscant mind;
And the blunt old Nehemiah,
  And Ezekiel refined!
Newly came the minor Prophets,
  Each with his distinctive robe.
Newly came the Song idyllic,
  And the tragedy of Job;
Deuteronomy the regal,
  To a towering mountain grew
With its comrade peaks around it—
  When I read the Bible through.

What a radiant procession,
  As the pages rise and fall;
James the sturdy, John the tender,
  O the myriad minded Paul!
Vast apocalyptic glories
  Wheel and thunder, flash and flame,
While the church triumphant raises
  One incomparable Name.
Ah, the story of the Saviour
  Never glows supremely true
Till you read it whole and swiftly,
  Till you read the Bible through.

You who like to play at Bible,
  Dip and dabble, here and there,
Just before you kneel aweary,
  And yawn through hurried prayer;
You who treat the Crown of Writings
  As you treat no other book—

CHRISTIAN LIVING

Just a paragraph disjointed,
    Just a crude, impatient look—
Try a worthier procedure,
    Try a broad and steady view;
You will kneel in very rapture
    When you read the Bible through!

—AMOS R. WELLS

AN OCTAVE OF VIRTUES

Mary Alice Biby

(NOTE.—Draw a harp on the blackboard. As the program is developed write on the various strings of the harp the virtues as mentioned.)

SOFT MUSIC: "Living for Jesus"

SONG: "Living for Jesus"

COMMENT (by superintendent): If we are going to live for Jesus, let us see what we are to do as found in our next song.

SONG: "Footsteps of Jesus"

DISCUSSION (led by the superintendent): Notice the words of the song just sung. What does following in the footsteps of Jesus give us? (Voluntary response.)

Light—light to walk with him; light to put into our lives every virtue he would have us acquire. I want us to think of an octave of virtues that Christ would have each of us put into our lives.

SCRIPTURE READING (read responsively by boys and girls): 2 Peter 1:1-12.

DISCUSSION (continued by the superintendent): Evidently Peter is talking to Christians. Do you believe in Christ? You cannot *add faith* until you have repented (changed) and believed in the Lord Jesus Christ. (Read Luke 13:3; John 3:16. Make a brief appeal.)

120

Suppose we consider this octave of virtues. What is an octave? (Voluntary response.) Yes, it is eight notes. Let us discuss the eight notes necessary to harmonize this octave of virtues that God would have us acquire.

(NOTE.—Ask all present to open their Bibles to 2 Peter 1 and at the top of the page write, "An Octave of Virtues." Suggest that each one underscore the verses as they are mentioned in the discussion.)

1. The first virtue mentioned is *faith*. When Noah went into the ark, what held him up? Was it his fear or the ark? It is not your fears but your faith in Jesus Christ that will hold you up.

CHORUS: "Only Believe"

DISCUSSION (continued by superintendent):

2. What is the second note as found in our Scripture? Yes, it is *virtue*. Pure and clean for Jesus' sake. If I take this clean white paper (illustrate as you talk) and drop some ink on it, what happens? Yes, it is soiled; I can take an ink eraser and remove most of the ink but what about the paper? (Voluntary response.) I can take a chemical and remove the ink but what about the paper? (Voluntary response.) Yes, there will be an ugly place in the paper. Its whiteness will be marred. So it is with the blackness of sin. The blood of Jesus Christ can cleanse you but there are some sins such as impurity that will leave blemishes in your lives that cannot be removed. They have left their mark.

3. What is the next virtue mentioned? (Voluntary response.) Yes, *knowledge*. What knowledge? Why? (Voluntary response.) (Discuss also the value of an education.)

4. The next note in this octave of virtues is *temperance* or *self-control*. Dr. P. E. Burroughs used to tell the following: "A stock show was in session. Exhibit after exhibit was shown and finally six big silver gray horses were driven into the ring. The driver with a look of pride on his face, ran them, galloped them, and walked them around the ring. All the time he had absolute control on the lines governing the horses. He pulled the lines to the right and all six of the horses turned. He pulled the lines to the left and again all six of the horses turned. He had absolute control on the lines." But I know of a control far greater than that. It is that control on the lines of life that enables an Intermediate to say no when he ought to say no, and to say yes when he ought to say yes.

5. Our next virtue is *patience*. How hard it is to get this note into our daily living but how important and what a blessing.

6. *Godliness* comes next. Seven days in the week. How may we acquire this? Yes, by looking at God daily through his Word and endeavoring to follow his pattern.

7. Then comes *brotherly kindness.*

8. This is followed by the eighth note *love.* Shall we all quote John 3:16? Love for God, for others, for God's cause.

QUESTION: Now we have a complete octave but what is necessary before an octave will produce music? It must be in tune. How can we tune this octave of virtues in our lives? Yes, through prayer and Bible study. But how are we to play this octave of virtues? That is true; we must *live* it from day to day. We must know the touch of the Master's hand on our daily lives.

POEM: THE TOUCH OF THE MASTER'S HAND

'Twas battered and scarred, and the auctioneer
    thought it scarcely worth his while
To waste much time on the old violin, but held
    it up with a smile;
"What am I bidden, good folks," he cried,
    "Who'll start the bidding for me?
A dollar, a dollar, now two, only two—
    Two dollars and who'll make it three?

"Three dollars once, three dollars twice,
    Going for three—but no . . ."
From the room far back, a gray-haired man
Came forward and picked up the bow;
Then wiping the dust from the old violin and
    tightening up all the strings,
He played a melody pure and sweet—as sweet
    as an angel sings.

123

The music ceased and the auctioneer
  With a voice that was quiet and low
Said, "What am I bidden for the old violin?"
  And he held it up with the bow.
"A thousand dollars and who'll make it two,
  Two thousand and who'll make it three?
Three thousand once, three thousand twice, and
  going and gone," said he.

The people cheered, but some of them cried,
  "We do not quite understand . . .
What changed its worth?" Swift came the reply
  "The touch of the Master's hand!"
And many a youth with a life out of tune, and
  battered and torn with sin
Is auctioned cheap to a thoughtless crowd much
  like the old violin.

A mess of pottage, a glass of wine,
  A game, and he travels on.
He is going once and going twice,
  He's going and almost gone.
But the Master comes and the foolish crowd
  Never can quite understand
The worth of a soul and the change that's wrought
  By the touch of the Master's hand.

—MYRA BROOKS WELCH, in *Illustrations from Art*,
published by Harper Brothers

INVENTORY SALE

Mrs. Lee MacDonell

(NOTE.—Place signs, "Inventory Sale," in the halls, on the stairway, at the entrance, and all about the assembly room.)

PRELUDE: "Nothing But the Blood"

DUET: "Whiter Than Snow"

SCRIPTURE READING: Matthew 5:48

QUOTATION: "The perfection spoken of is the perfection of love, the supreme virtue of God and man."

—DUMMELOW

SENTENCE PRAYERS (Have the pianist play softly during these prayers): "Whiter Than Snow"

DISCUSSION (led by the superintendent): While walking downtown the other morning, I saw a large sign across a store something like this, "Inventory Sale." What is meant by an inventory? Why is an inventory taken? What does it mean to a store? (Voluntary responses.)

I walked into the store and looking around I saw a number of tables. Going over to one I found this sign, *Odd Sizes*. Odd sizes? I began thinking. These are not regular sizes but odd sizes. In our lives we have odd sizes too, such as faults and bad habits. They don't fit anywhere. (Ask pupils to name some, which may include gossip, worry, cheating, deceit, and so on.)

125

I have given each of you a paper and pencil. Please take an inventory of yourself in the presence of God without letting anyone know what you write, and put on this paper one fault or one bad habit which you are willing to put on sale—one that you will try hard to dispose of. Thank you! Now will you place them on this table marked "Odd Sizes"? (Soft music, "Whiter Than Snow" may be played as this is being done.)

PRAYER: that God will help each one to dispose of the fault or bad habit designated

DISCUSSION (continued by the superintendent): I next walked over to a table marked, *Remnants.* These remnants are typical of good resolutions unkept. Many of us have a number of these on hand.

How would you look in a dress or suit you wore when you were eight years old? Yet many are still clinging to habits formed years ago. You resolve to break yourself of a habit, but the good resolution is still on hand unkept.

Again will you take an inventory of your life and see what broken resolution you want to rid yourself of?

There was another table piled high with merchandise which was labeled, *Slightly Soiled.* Let us take an inventory of ourselves for the third time. What do we find? Sightly soiled hands—used for

126

wrong purposes. Slightly soiled lips—lies, oaths, gossip, smutty stories.

Slightly soiled mind—impure thoughts

Slightly soiled body—impurity, smoking, drinking, neglect

I enjoyed the inventory sale, but found nothing I needed. So, too, this morning as you have looked over the odd sizes, remnants, and slightly soiled things of your life you have found nothing you need. May God help each of you to make the inventory taken a profitable one.

PRAYER: that each one may put the slightly soiled and other hindering things out of his life

LIFE'S PLAN SHEET

Mrs. C. H. Cosby

Soft Music: "Living for Jesus" (piano and violin)

Song: "Trust and Obey"

Discussion (by the superintendent): "Looking at Self"

Have you ever fallen out with yourself because you found that you were hard to manage? You plan to do so many things which you never find time to do and sometimes find your days all in a muddle so that even life itself seems in a tangle. All of you who are really trying to make your life worth while have to call a halt now and then, check your plans, and see where you are headed. It is a good plan to budget your time and balance your program.

(Note.—Draw a large face of a clock on the blackboard and mark it off into twenty-four hours instead of twelve.)

You notice I have put a time chart on the board. It is a copy of one found hanging over the desk of a college student. I suggest that each of you make a time chart for your room at home and then divide your time into sections of work, play, study, service, sleep, eating, reading, and recreation. You, yourself, will decide how you will invest your twenty-four hours.

128

But God gives us more than a day; he gives each of us a lifetime. We do not know how many years we are to have, but we do know that all the years we have lived, added to all the years we may yet live, make up our lifetime. So I am going to erase the face of the clock and leave the circle marked "Life." (Erase all but circle.)

Now, tell me some of the things you want to do during your life and I will list them on the board. (Voluntary response.) Yes, there is much to do and we do not want to get frustrated, so let us arrange a plan sheet by which we may shape all our living. I am going to divide the circle into three sections and then name them as you read out of God's Word.

(NOTE.—Write the following references on slips of paper and give them to nine pupils before the program begins. Write the three phrases in the sections of the circle during the opening strain of each song. There should be no announcement of the special music.)

1. *Search His Word*—Mark 13:31; John 5:39; Psalm 119:11.

SOLO (first stanza): "Wonderful Words of Life"

2. *Seek His Will*—Psalm 143:10; Proverbs 3:5-6; Matthew 16:24.

DUET (first stanza): "Have Thine Own Way, Lord"

3. *Spread His Love*—John 14:23; Matthew 28:18-20; Acts 1:8.

SONG (first and third stanzas): "I Love to Tell the Story"

129

CLOSING APPEAL (by the superintendent): Would not you like to join me in this life plan that together we may "search his Word" as "we see his will" that we may truly "spread his love" each day as long as we shall live?

SENTENCE PRAYERS

THE LORD'S DAY

Mary Virginia Lee

PRELUDE (played softly): "Nearer, Still Nearer"

SONG: "Safely Through Another Week"

PRAYER: of gratitude

STORY (by the superintendent): "The Seven Chests"

(NOTE.—Have a poster or drawing on blackboard of seven chests.)

Long ago a very kind father, who dearly loved his children, tried to think of a way in which to make them all happy. One day, calling them to him, he said, "Come with me, my children, into the treasure house."

Great was their delight as they gazed upon the dazzling gems which were displayed in seven magnificent caskets. Still greater was their joy when their father said, pointing to six of the caskets which stood in a row, "From each of these six caskets each of you may select a jewel, which shall be yours to do with as you will. Only the jewels in the seventh casket, yonder, shall I keep for my own."

When each son and each daughter had carefully chosen a gem from each of the six caskets they turned to go. Some thanked the father for his generous gift, and told him they were going to use his

131

jewels to make him glad, and the father's eyes kindled in loving joy. But some were already busily planning how they would use their jewels to gain money and pleasure and ease for themselves alone. As they turned away with not so much as a word of gratitude, the father's face clouded with disappointment.

Then a sad thing happened. Some of the ungrateful sons and daughters, not content with their share of the jewels, whispered among themselves: "These jewels are not enough to bring us all the pleasure and wealth we want. Let us go secretly to our father's treasure house and take jewels from that seventh casket."

So, while the grateful sons and daughters were enjoying their jewels and the generosity of their father, the ungrateful ones were creeping stealthily back to the treasure house. Noiselessly they stretched out their hands and each stole a jewel from their father's share.

But the father knew what those sons and daughters had done and his gracious heart was grieved that the children whom he loved could treat him so.

You have probably already guessed that this is a parable, that the chests represent days of the week. We are the children and the father is our Lord. Have you ever been guilty of taking from the Lord's Day? Of using it for your own?

EXPLANATION OF THE LORD'S DAY (by the superintendent): In the very beginning, God set aside and hallowed the seventh day as a day of rest and worship. Moses gave very strict rules for its observance. One of the Ten Commandments was concerning it. Who can repeat it? ("Remember the sabbath day to keep it holy" Exodus 20:8.) It was Jesus' custom to go to the synagogue on the sabbath and there discuss the Scriptures and heal the lame.

After Jesus' death and resurrection, the disciples met on the first day of the week for worship and preaching (Acts 20:7). This day soon became known among Christ's followers as the Lord's Day; thus, the first day of the week became the Christian's sabbath.

DISCUSSION (by the superintendent): "How Should We Observe the Lord's Day?"

1. As a day of rest, when man shall cease from his routine labor. Leviticus 16:31.

2. As a holy day when man shall worship God. Exodus 20:8; Isaiah 66:23; Acts 20:7; 1 Corinthians 16:1-2.

3. As a day for rejoicing when man shall be happy. Psalm 118:24.

4. As a day for studying God's Word when man shall teach and study it.

133

5. As a day for preaching when man shall preach and hear preaching. Acts 13:42-44.

6. As a day for Christian fellowship, when Christians shall assemble together. Acts 16:13.

7. As a day of service, when man shall render special service unto his Lord. Matthew 12:12.

You may often wonder, "Is it wrong to do this or that on Sunday?" Then ask yourself this question, "Would it please God?"

Remember that it is the Lord's Day and not ours. Therefore, we should please him and not ourselves.

STORY (by the superintendent): "The Lord's Day"

It was Sunday afternoon. Ralph had been to Sunday school and preaching. Now that dinner was over, he wanted to go to the picture show, but his father objected to Sunday movies and forbade his going.

Mother had suggested several things for him to do. One was that he call some of his friends and that they go over to see James who was a shut-in because of a broken leg. But Ralph had his heart set on going to the show.

"I don't like Sunday anyway," he muttered. "I wish there was no such thing as a Lord's Day," he said with such feeling that Grandfather, who was sitting by the window reading his Bible, suddenly looked up with an expression of alarm and said, "My son, don't say those words again. They make me afraid."

"Afraid? What do you mean, Grandfather?" Ralph asked.

"Come here, I want to tell you a story," said Grandfather. Ralph went over and sat at his grandfather's knees.

"Years ago, when I was only a lad like you, I did not like to go to church. I was not a Christian, and the worship of the Lord meant nothing to me. But I had a good mother who loved God and his church, and she insisted that I go whether I wanted to or not. The months went by, and I grew more and more rebellious. Then one Sunday morning I was angry. I hated the church; I hated everything. In stubborn determination, I turned in the road and said to my mother, "Mother, this is the last time I am ever going to church. I wish I lived in a world without churches. I wish every church on earth would close and never open again. I wish there was no such a day as Sunday."

That night I dreamed a terrible dream. I thought that a messenger from God stood by my bed and commanded me to follow him. He took me to a land in which there were no Lord's Day nor churches! He took me there, and without a word left me alone in that awful land.

I cannot tell you all the things I saw and heard in that land, but as I walked in terror up and down the streets, there were sick people lying all along the way, begging for relief from pain. When I urged someone to call a doctor, they answered, "There are no doctors here, and there are no hospitals. Doctors and hospitals are only found in the land of churches."

Thousands of little children were crying in the streets, begging for food and a place of rest. But when I asked about them, I was told that they were orphan children and that there was nobody to care for them, because they were living in a land that did not recognize God.

All along the way I saw men and women with sin written in their faces, and with heavy burdens on their backs. They were lost people, for there was no church and no pastor to tell them of Jesus. They were men and women without hope in the world.

When I had looked upon sin and suffering and sorrow until I felt I could stand no more, suddenly I fell on my face in that awful land without a church or a Lord's Day and cried: "Oh, God, if you'll take me back to the land where the churches are, I'll give my life to you, and I shall love your house and your day as long as I live. Week by week I shall worship in it, and all the years you give me, I shall spend in your service."

My prayer was scarcely uttered before I felt a gentle touch on my shoulder: the messenger of God was standing by and an angel chorus was singing a beautiful song —"Day of All the Week the Best."

I awoke to find myself in a land of churches and ever since I have been happy when the Lord's Day comes.

Silence. A young boy was seeing through an old man's eyes the dream of an old man's youth.

Quietly he arose. "Grandpa, let's be going. It is time for the service to begin, and we must not be late."

—S. T. C., in *The Intermediate Leader*.
Used by permission.

PRAYER: of gratitude for the Lord's Day

SONG (first and second stanzas): "Take Time to Be Holy"

TEST YOUR AMUSEMENTS

Clara Mae Macke

(NOTE.—Ask several capable boys and girls with two alert adults to sit around a table and carry out this program in conversational manner. Adults will merely guide the panel.)

SOLO: "I Would Be True"

SONG (first and second stanzas): "Nothing Between"

PRAYER (bow heads and sing softly second and third stanzas): "Nearer, Still Nearer"

PANEL DISCUSSION

Question: Some of the gang go to the dances, drink, and do other things and have the best time. My folks won't let me and I simply don't see why. Will someone explain?

Answer: Suppose we find what God would have us do. Psalm 119:9-16; Psalm 119:33-37. You know, I don't believe I can drink and dance and still keep those vows. I wonder if we can find some real tests for our amusements.

Test number one. Will this that I am about to do make me stronger in body, mind, and soul? Let me see now, will drinking, dancing, smoking, and other questionable amusements make me stronger in body, mind, and soul?

Test number two. Will these amusements make me really happy? There are many things we might do in life but they do not satisfy our souls.

Test number three. These first two questions may be applied to any person whether he is a Christian or not. But the Christian should go even further. Will this amusement hurt me? Will it hurt my influence? Will it glorify God?

A young lady who was converted asked her pastor if she could not dance, as she felt sure it was all right. He said, "Go, if you feel that you can serve your Master and if you can while there ask your partner if he is a Christian." The girl was sure that she could, so went to the dance. But she found it very difficult to ask her partner about his soul. However, she felt she must keep her word, so late in the evening she said to him, "Are you a Christian?" "No," he said in a very surprised tone, "are you?" "Yes," she replied slowly. "Then what in the world are you doing here?" was his question.

—The Christian Index. Used by permission.

SONG (first stanza and chorus): "My Desire"

Answer (continued): Suppose we turn to God's Word for further help on the solution of this problem.

(NOTE.—References should be previously assigned. Call for Ephesians 5:22; Joshua 24:15; Proverbs 21:17; Isaiah 58:13, 14; 1 Timothy 5:6; 3 John 4, 11; Ephesians 5:11; 2 Corinthians 6:17-18.)

Question: What are some of the most common amusements that Intermediates are concerned about? (Answered by several of the panel.)

CHRISTIAN LIVING

As you think of these amusements will they pass the tests that we have discussed?

CONCLUSION (by superintendent): Uncle Tom in *The Christian Index* says: "Make your pleasures a matter of prayer. To those of you who ask me, 'May I do this? Shall I do that? Can I go there?' I reply: 'Have you prayed about it?' The boy or girl who is sufficiently in earnest touching anything in his or her life about which there is a question, to make it a real matter of prayer will, I feel sure, get a definite answer as to the course to be pursued."

I heard a good story some time ago about a girl who was staying with an aunt away from her home. While there, she received an invitation to go to a dance. She had an idea that her mother would not approve of her going, so she told her aunt about her difficulty. Thoughtfully the reply was given: "Phyllis, let us make it a matter of prayer?" Instantly the girl responded: "Oh, don't say that; don't pray about it; for if you do, I know I shall not get to the party!" You see the point!

If you love the Saviour with all your heart, if you are determined to live for him you will gladly obey his voice regardless of the price to be paid. You will willingly forego any so-called pleasure when you know there is a question mark attached. The Mas-

139

ter knows the things that will prove harmful to you and to your influence and will strengthen you against them and lead you into every day deeds of usefulness if you will heed his voice. Will you do it?

(*Suggestion:* It would be splendid to appoint a committee to meet with the song leader and chairman of activities to work out a schedule of recreational projects.)

SONG: "Living for Jesus"

PRAYER

GOD'S RECIPES

R. L. Middleton

SONG: "My Desire"

DISCUSSION (led by superintendent):

During the days when food was being rationed, housewives found it difficult to secure various grocery items, meats, etc., and to make their different kinds of points go as far as possible. They faced many problems and had to be quite ingenious in preparing their meals.

In the good old days when meats and groceries and vegetables were plentiful, the housewife found great delight in trying out different kinds of recipes. Nearly every good housewife has different kinds of cookbooks, boxes for recipes, and the like. (Have some on display.) Then too she is constantly searching the newspapers, reading the magazines, and listening to the radio for new recipes sponsored by different manufacturers of flour, flavoring extracts, and gelatine manufacturers.

From some current magazines I have clipped some attractive advertisements in which are illustrated the results obtained by following certain recipes. For instance, here is a recipe for— (The superintendent should cut full page advertisements from

141

magazines and paste them on some cardboards about twelve by fourteen inches. Hold up or refer in some way to the poster on which the ads and recipes are given.)

Each one of these recipes is enough to make any of us hungry.

Famous chefs have made certain hotels and restaurants throughout the country famous by their own secret recipes. Duncan Hines has traveled throughout our country finding unusually good eating places and has listed them for the benefit of the people. These restaurants, cafeterias and other eating places take great pride in having a recommendation from Duncan Hines. (The Leader might mention some local eating place that is famous or well known for its pies or cakes or steaks, etc.)

A Kansas City schoolteacher took a vacation trip to New York City and enjoyed some delicious cake and icing at a widely known Manhattan hotel.

Returning home, she wrote to the hotel and asked for the recipes, concluding: "Naturally, I am willing to pay for them."

She received the recipes by return mail, with a bill for one hundred dollars enclosed.

A lawyer advised her to pay. She did.

Yes, some recipes come high but there are recipes available to each of us that are free. In fact, copies of these choice recipes may be had without cost. I refer to the Bible and "God's Recipes."

Suppose we take a dozen of God's recipes and see how he has provided for us in so many ways. May we take these up in the following order. (Call for these to be read by individuals or responsively by the group and make some brief comment after each one.)

1. For Salvation:

For God so loved the world, that he gave his only begotten Son, that whosoever believeth in him should not perish, but have everlasting life. For God sent not his Son into the world to condemn the world; but that the world through him might be saved. He that believeth on him is not condemned: but he that believeth not is condemned already, because he hath not believed in the name of the only begotten Son of God (John 3:16-18).

2. For Eternal Life:

He that believeth on the Son hath everlasting life: and he that believeth not the Son shall not see life; but the wrath of God abideth on him (John 3:36).

3. For Sabbath Observance:

And on the seventh day God ended his work which he had made; and he rested on the seventh day from all his work which he had made (Gen. 2:2).

Remember the sabbath day, to keep it holy. Six days shalt thou labour, and do all thy work: But the seventh day is the sabbath of the Lord thy God: in it thou shalt not do any work, thou nor thy son nor thy daughter, thy manservant nor thy maidservant, nor thy cattle, nor thy stranger that is within thy gates: for in six days the Lord made heaven and earth, the sea, and all that in them is, and rested the seventh day: wherefore the Lord blessed the sabbath day, and hallowed it (Ex. 20:8-11).

4. For Discipleship:

Then said Jesus to those Jews which believed on him, If ye continue in my word, then are ye my disciples indeed (John 8:31).

By this shall all men know that ye are my disciples, if ye have love one to another (John 13:35).

And he shall be like a tree planted by the rivers of water, that bringeth forth his fruit in his season; his leaf also shall not wither; and whatsoever he doeth shall prosper (Psalm 1:3).

5. For Abundant and Fruitful Life:

I am the true vine, and my Father is the husbandman. Every branch in me that beareth not fruit he taketh away: and every branch that beareth fruit, he purgeth it, that it may bring forth more fruit. Now ye are clean through the word which I have spoken unto you. Abide in me, and I in you. As the branch cannot bear fruit of itself, except it abide in the vine; no more can ye, except ye abide in me. I am the vine, ye are the branches: He that abideth in me, and I in him, the same bringeth forth much fruit: for without me ye can do nothing (John 15:1-5).

144

COMMENTS (by superintendent):

Our fruitage for Christ reveals our rootage in him.

Our lives must take deep rootage in Christ to bear rich fruitage for Christ.

6. For Guidance:

Trust in the Lord with all thine heart; and lean not unto thine own understanding. In all thy ways acknowledge him, and he shall direct thy paths (Prov. 3:5-6).

7. For Greatness:

But it shall not be so among you: but whosoever will be great among you, let him be your minister; And whosoever will be chief among you, let him be your servant: Even as the Son of Man came not to be ministered unto, but to minister, and to give his life a ransom for many (Matt. 20:26-28).

8. For Happiness:

Psalm 1:1-6. Substitute the word "happy" for the word "blessed" in the opening sentence. The word blessed is often translated happy.

(Since some may not have their Bibles, this Psalm is quite often found in responsive readings of hymnbooks and if it is available this serves a good opportunity for the entire department to read responsively or it can be assigned as the other Scriptures.)

9. For Praise:

It is a good thing to give thanks unto the Lord, and to sing praise unto thy name, O most High (Psalm 92:1).

Praise ye the Lord. O give thanks unto the Lord; for he is good: for his mercy endureth for ever (Psalm 106:1).

10. For the Hungry:

And Jesus said unto them, I am the bread of life: he that cometh to me shall never hunger; and he that believeth on me shall never thirst (John 6:35).

11. For a Happy Nation:

Righteousness exalteth a nation: but sin is a reproach to any people (Prov. 14:34).

Blessed is the nation whose God is the Lord; and the people whom he hath chosen for his own inheritance (Psalm 33:12).

12. For Wisdom:

If any of you lack wisdom, let him ask of God, that giveth to all men liberally, and upbraideth not; and it shall be given him. But let him ask in faith, nothing wavering. For he that wavereth is like a wave of the sea driven with the wind and tossed (James 1:5-6).

CONCLUSION (by superintendent):

From these Scriptures we need never worry about spiritual food. God's Word has never been rationed and we hope it never will be. It is available for all of us at all times and we should covet the privilege of using it every day—"Thy word have I hid in my heart that I might not sin against thee."

You cannot form a better habit and one that will give you greater satisfaction than the habit of using

"God's Recipes" for your guidance in your daily living.

HOLY BIBLE, BOOK DIVINE

Holy Bible, Book divine, Precious treasure, thou
    art mine;

Mine to tell me whence I came; Mine to teach
    me what I am;

Mine to chide me when I rove; Mine to show
    a Saviour's love;

Mine thou art to guide and guard; Mine to
    punish or reward;

Mine to comfort in distress, Suffering in this
    wilderness;

Mine to show, by living faith, Man can triumph
    over death;

Mine to tell of joys to come, And the rebel sin-
    ner's doom;

O thou holy Book divine, Precious treasure,
    thou art mine.

—JOHN BURTON, in *The Broadman Hymnal*

PRAYER

HOBBIES

Robert Aides

(NOTE.—Display folders on various hobbies, especially the ones mentioned in this program.)

VIOLIN SOLO (ask the department to hum the last stanza, a soloist singing the question, "What hast thou brought to Me?"): "I Gave My Life for Thee"

SOLO: "Take My Life, and Let It Be"

QUESTION (by the superintendent): What kind of people do you admire most? What kind of person do you want to be when you are grown? (Lead the suggestion to an "all-round person.") What do we mean when we say a person is the "best all-round?" (Voluntary response.) An all-round person is one who endeavors to utilize every gift that is within him. He did not become "all-round" over night, however but early in life he learned how to make every moment count. In his life there are few wasted moments.

SONG (first stanza): "To the Work"

DISCUSSION (led by the superintendent): I once heard of an organization of Minute Men—men who pledged to employ every minute of the day usefully. In the day there are twenty-four hours of opportunities. I wonder how you boys and girls spend those hours?

148

(NOTE.—Draw a large circle on a piece of poster board and cut this circle into twenty-four segments [representing twenty-four hours] each piece bearing a number from 1 to 24. Write on each piece how that particular hour is spent [for example: Sleep, chores, study, school, etc.] As the distribution will differ in various localities, the leader should mark the distribution of time beforehand. Two segments are left blank. One at a time ask each of the twenty-four pupils to bring his segment of the circle to the front. Arrange them in order on the blackboard.)

DISCUSSION (continued by the superintendent): This is a division of the average Intermediate's day and in it I notice two unfilled hours. What do you do in those two hours? (Some suggest picture shows, reading, "just go down town," and the like.) Some folk think of hobbies merely as things like collecting stamps and autographs, and that they are only for shut-ins and stay-at-homes. However, their idea is wrong. Hobbies represent what you are most keenly interested in. A hobby should furnish *fun and enjoyment*, be *instructive*, require *skill* and *proficiency*, and develop mentally, physically, and socially. (Write the words that are set in italics on the blackboard.) I have asked several of our boys and girls to tell us about some hobbies that meet these requirements.

1. *Gardening.*—Flowers and shrubbery may be set out in the yard at home. Rock gardens may be made. Vegetables may be planted. Later in the season these flowers and vegetables may be shared with others.

2. *Painting.*—Many girls like to paint things such as vases, jars, and jugs. Inexpensive articles may be

purchased at novelty stores to paint. Often they paint vases and waste baskets for their Sunday school classrooms. I am sure boys must like to paint also—perhaps porch furniture, flower boxes, and many such things.

3. *Golf.*—I think golf is a good hobby for it gives one plenty of exercise and keeps him out in the fresh air. It also affords fine fellowship with others.

4. *Domestic Science.*—This is a practical as well as useful hobby which aids one in learning to cook and sew. Girls who are experienced often assist their domestic science teacher, and they frequently conduct classes in mill sections for girls who are interested in learning to cook and sew. Some make all their clothes; they also make attractive gifts for others.

5. *Photography.*—This is a fascinating hobby. It affords much real enjoyment and helps one to spend many hours in the open. Some boys and girls are making a collection of pictures of wild-life animals, birds, trees, and flowers. Others are making a collection of beautiful scenes.

6. *Woodwork.*—Some boys have shops in their garages or basements where they make various pieces of furniture, whatnots, boats, airplanes Often they sell the things they make and use the money to buy more tools and material to work with.

7. *Interviewing Interesting People.*—This is a hobby that appeals to both boys and girls. They make the acquaintance of many outstanding people, and keep scrapbooks of their interviews. This type of hobby helps one know how to meet the people, and it is certainly good for developing one's personality and character.

CLOSING DISCUSSION (led by the superintendent): Please name some other hobbies that meet the requirements which are listed on the blackboard. (Voluntary response.) I'm sure all of us agree that hobbies are interesting. In what ways are they beneficial? (Voluntary response such as: Keep one out of mischief; furnish recreation and entertainment; often help one to decide on his vocation; self improvement.) What may have been Jesus' hobby when a boy? (Working in his father's carpenter shop.) Is there a verse in the Bible to prove that he must have benefited from this employment of leisure time? (All stand and read Luke 2:52.) Having given your heart to him and with a wise investment of time, you, like Jesus, may increase "in wisdom and stature, and in favour with God and man." You can be an "all-round person."

SONG: "Give of Your Best to the Master"

PRAYER

STEWARDSHIP

Mrs. M. T. Crabtree

SOFT MUSIC: "I Surrender All"

SONG: "Wherever He Leads I'll Go"

CALL TO WORSHIP: "The Lord is in his holy temple: let all the earth keep silence before him" (Hab. 2:20).

SONG: "Make Me a Channel of Blessing"

SCRIPTURE READING: Luke 12:42-48

DISCUSSION (led by the superintendent): Today Southern Baptists teach a great deal about Stewardship. What does it mean to be a steward? (Voluntary response.) Suppose Mary gives the dictionary definition for a steward. Yes, one entrusted with the affairs of another. As a Christian you have the responsibility of being a steward; for Jesus Christ has left the affairs of his kingdom in the Christian's hands.

You Intermediates have many things entrusted to you as stewards of Jesus Christ. This morning as we sing let us take an inventory of our stewardship.

SONG (first stanza): "Take My Life, and Let It Be"

BRIEF TALK: "Stewards of Life" (1 Cor. 6:9-10)

SONG (second stanza): "Take My Life, and Let It Be"

BRIEF TALK: "Stewards of Our Talents" (Eph. 4:11-12)

SONG (third stanza): "Take My Life, and Let It Be"

BRIEF TALK: "Stewards of Our Money" (Mal. 3: 10)

BRIEF TALK: "Stewards of Our Time" (Psalm 90:12)

SCRIPTURE READING: 2 Corinthians 8:5

DISCUSSION (by the superintendent): The gift of self is the highest and noblest gift that you can make to the Lord. No one can become a Christian without surrendering his life to Christ. Then in giving your self, you will gladly give your possessions—your talents, time, and money. If you have not taken Christ into your heart, now is the time to take him as your Saviour and become a steward in his kingdom. Will you who have not done so think seriously of this matter as we sing?

SONG (fourth stanza): "Take My Life, and Let It Be"

CONCLUSION (by the superintendent): If you would be a faithful steward you will study your

Bible to learn God's will and then pray for grace to obey it. The faithful steward will receive a reward (Matt. 25:21).

SONG: "Trust, Try, and Prove Me"

IT IS MORE BLESSED TO GIVE
(Tithing)

Mrs. Myrtle Creasman

(NOTE.—Hand a pamphlet on tithing to each one as he enters. Display pamphlets, posters, and Scripture reference on tithing.)

SONG (have group entering from the back singing first stanza and chorus): "Trust, Try, and Prove Me"

ILLUSTRATION (by the superintendent): It is recorded of that Christian soldier, Stonewall Jackson, how, from the thick of the second Bull Run battle, he sent a letter to his pastor back at home containing this passage: "I remember that next sabbath is the day upon which the collection is taken for foreign missions. Enclosed find my check."

CHORUS: "Trust, Try, and Prove Me"

SCRIPTURE READING (read by the department): Acts 20:35

DISCUSSION (by the superintendent; showing a poster with the word "Blessed"): The word "blessed" means happy. Do you really believe that you are happier when you give than when you receive? The first step in Christian giving is tithing. Really we cannot truly call tithing giving for the tithe belongs to God and so is a debt that we pay and not a gift that we give. Suppose we find why

155

Jackson was blessed by giving; why it is more blessed to give than to receive.

1. *Tithing is obedience.*—Tithing is a blessing because it is obedience to God's command. In Malachi 3:10a God says: "Bring ye all the tithes into the storehouse." Therefore, those who claim to be his children must do it. Only those who obey God are truly happy. "Blessed are they that hear the Word of God, and keep it" (Luke 11:28).

2. *Tithing is a part of good stewardship.*—Tithing is a blessing because it is a part of good stewardship. God is the owner of all things. "The earth is the Lord's, and the fullness thereof; the world and they that dwell therein" (Psalm 24:1). Since God owns us and all that we have then we are his stewards entrusted with his property to use to his glory. And he requires that for the use of his possessions we shall pay him one-tenth of all he gives us. This is the first step in the stewardship of possessions. "Moreover it is required in stewards, that a man be found faithful" (1 Cor. 4:2). Only faithful stewards can be truly happy.

3. *Tithing meets financial needs.*—Tithing is a blessing because it meets financial needs of God's kingdom. If all Christians tithed there would be money in abundance for every kingdom enterprise. The tithes of Southern Baptists would be about two hundred million dollars a year, enough for the gen-

erous support of every local church and to meet every need of our benevolent and missionary causes.

CHORUS: "Send the Light"

4. *Tithing brings blessings.*—Tithing brings the greatest blessings to the tithers. Like all of God's laws, the law of the tithe is for the benefit of those obeying it.

CHORUS (concealed voices): "Trust, Try, and Prove Me"

SCRIPTURE READING (concealed voice): "Prove me now herewith, saith the Lord of hosts, if I will not open you the windows of heaven, and pour you out a blessing, that there shall not be room enough to receive it" (Mal. 3:10).

COMMENT (by the superintendent): This is God's promise to faithful tithers. The experience of thousands of tithers proves that God does bless those who tithe with both material and spiritual blessings.

TESTIMONY: "I know God blesses tithers"

(NOTE.—Display a poster featuring giving)

DISCUSSION (by the superintendent): "Tithing Is Not Sufficient"

God expects his people not only to pay tithes, but to give gifts. Tithers always want to give gifts over and above the tithe.

1. *Giving completes our stewardship.*—Giving is a blessing because it completes our faithful stewardship of possessions. God commands and expects us to give and we can rob him in offerings as well as in tithes. Therefore we cannot claim to be faithful stewards until we add to our tithes our free will offering.

2. *Giving is an expression of love.*—Giving is a blessing because it is our expression of love. Lovers are always givers. The more we love God the more we want to give to him. The tithe belongs to him. After that is paid we ought to prove our love for God with a free will offering from our nine-tenths. "Freely ye have received, freely give" (Matt. 10:8).

3. *Giving brings blessings to God's work.*—Kingdom causes need our gifts as well as our tithes. Our tithe should go into the Lord's treasury regularly each Lord's Day as we have prospered. Often there are special needs that make it necessary to call for special gifts. Then we have the opportunity of showing our love by these gifts and so bring special blessings to the Lord's work.

STORY (by superintendent):

A merchant, at his own expense supported several native missionaries in India and gave liberally to the cause of Christ at home. On being asked how he could afford to do it, he replied, "Before my conversion, when I served the world and self, I did it on a grand scale, at the most

158

lavish expense. And when God by his grace called me out of darkness, I resolved that Christ and his cause should have more than I ever spent in the world. And as to giving so much, it is God who enables me to do it; for at my conversion I promised that I would give to his cause a fixed proportion of all that my business brought in to me. Every year since I made that promise, it has brought in about double what it did the year before, so that I easily can, as I do, double my gifts for his service."

—From *625 New Bible Stories and Scripture Anecdotes*. George W. Noble, Publisher, Chicago, Illinois. (Used by permission.)

4. *Giving blesses the giver.*—"Give and it shall be given unto you; good measure, pressed down, and shaken together, and running over, shall men give into your bosom. For with the same measure that ye mete withal it shall be measured to you again" (Luke 6:38).

(NOTE.—Continue to display the poster on "Giving" throughout the next number.)

DUET (first and third stanzas): "I Gave My Life for Thee"

DISCUSSION (by the superintendent showing a poster marked "Blessed"): "The Beatitudes of Giving"

Blessed are the givers, for they shall receive gifts from God.

Blessed are the generous givers, for their souls shall be made fat.

159

Blessed are the cheerful givers, for they shall have the love of God.

Blessed are they who give themselves, for they are like Jesus.

Indeed, "it is more blessed to give than to receive" (Acts 20:35).

PRAYER: that God will help each one to resolve to take him at his word and become a tither and thus insure the blessings of God upon his life as well as contribute to the great program of evangelizing a lost world

CHORUS: "Trust, Try, and Prove Me"

MY LIFE FOR JESUS

WHAT SHALL I DO WITH MY LIFE?

Fannie Mae Wright

PLAYLET

CHARACTERS

IRENE, *attractive sixteen-year girl representing an unsaved girl*

JUANITA, *a gaily dressed girl, caring only for herself and worldly things*

CHRISTINE, *a truly consecrated girl dressed in white*

SINGER

SCENE

GARDEN SCENE. *Porch or garden furniture, ferns, and other potted plants may be used.* IRENE *is seated in one of the chairs reading a magazine. Soft music, "Think On Thy Way," is heard.*

IRENE: I wish I knew what to do with my life. I just can't decide. I have talents to use in some way; I have a heart to give for something. Surely, I can render service for some cause. How I wish someone would show me what to do!

JUANITA: (*Enters with a globe of the world in her hand.*) Hello there, Irene; what's your trouble?

163

IRENE: Oh, I'm trying to decide what to do with my life.

JUANITA: That will be easy to decide. I've been searching for another girl to join in with the world. We have the gayest crowd you ever saw. We certainly could use a girl just like you. With your charming personality and your many talents, you would make a big hit in the gang. You would be popular to the last degree. Come on; bring your talents along and join the world!

IRENE: That sounds fine, Juanita, but what would I do with my heart and how would I serve? You spoke only of my talents.

JUANITA: Oh, we of the world forget about such things as that. That's old-fashioned talk, Irene. Your heart is just an organ of your body that keeps the blood circulating.

IRENE: That's true, but you know what I meant. I was thinking of the heart as the psalmist did. I suppose in today's language we would say the mind. Anyway, it would be a hard thing to forget.

JUANITA: Oh, we will help you forget. And as for service, we worldly people don't have to worry about anyone's welfare but our own. Everyone looks out for himself and is kept busy with the job. You won't find any time to bother with other folk. We generally go from evening till morning at high speed and sleep during the day. I'm on my way now to help plan a party. (*Looks at watch.*) Gee, I'll be late if I don't hurry. (*Starts to leave but turns back as she gets to the door.*) I will leave this globe with you so that you can think more about it. Don't tax your brain too much; just remember, we live in a whirl of pleasure. So long! I'll be seeing you.

(*Exit* JUANITA. IRENE *remains and seems to be thinking very seriously. She hears soft music and listens. Then off stage a clear voice sings the first stanza of "Think On Thy Way.")*

SINGER: Think on thy way, O thou storm-driven child;

Out on the ocean so dark and so wild,

Far from thy God you are drifting to-day,—

Think on thy way, think on thy way.

IRENE: I am a "storm-driven child," and the life Juanita offers does not seem to calm the tempest within. (*The voice sings again*):

SINGER: Think on thy way: without Pilot or Guide,

Far from the shore with no Friend by your side,

Thoughtless of Him who would fain be your stay,

Think on thy way, think on thy way.

165

IRENE: I wish someone would help me find that Pilot. I just can't understand all of this. (*Voice sings*):

SINGER: Think on thy way, God will not let you go;

His mighty arm can destroy ev'ry foe;

Trust Him today, all his mandates obey;

Think on thy way, think on thy way.

(Copyright, 1917. E. O. Excell)

CHRISTINE: (*Entering*) Oh, my friend, you look lonely.

IRENE: I am lonely, but why do you call me friend? We've never met before.

CHRISTINE: No, but we can be friends, can't we? Our Master taught us to be friends to all people. What has been worrying you?

IRENE: I don't know what to do with my life. Can you help me? You seem to be so happy. Surely you have selected the right course.

CHRISTINE: I'll be glad to help you. What have you considered doing with your life, may I ask?

IRENE: Before I talked with Juanita, a friend of mine, I felt that I had a heart to give for something and talents to use in some way, and that I should be able to render service for some cause.

CHRISTINE: You are a wise girl, Irene. You surely have all those, and I can help you satisfy your desire. How would you like to give your heart to one who died for you?

IRENE: Oh, I would love to do that if it were possible, but how can I give my heart to one who is dead?

CHRISTINE: That is the glorious part of it. He isn't dead; he is risen. He conquered the grave and lives again. Listen. Those songs will explain.

(*A concealed voice sings the first stanza of "The Old Rugged Cross."* IRENE *and* CHRISTINE *remain silent with bowed heads; then the voice sings the first stanza of "Christ Arose."*)

IRENE: I do understand. I do want to give my heart to Christ, because I believe in him. I know he died for my sins. But you said you would tell me how to use my talents.

CHRISTINE: I am so happy to know that you will give your heart to Jesus. You may use your talents in a splendid way for him. He commanded that those who trust him should follow him in baptism and become members of the church. There in his church you may use your talents and serve him in a great way.

IRENE: But there is still one thing that isn't clear. Isn't there some place in your plan for the world? I'd like to help Juanita and her crowd. Their lives seem so empty. Can't we help them?

CHRISTINE: Indeed we can. Jesus said, "Go ye into all the world, and preach the gospel to every creature."

IRENE: Oh, I am so glad he included the world.

CHRISTINE: But, Irene, you must be apart from the world. You must serve it but be apart from it.

IRENE: I shall be glad to. I want to give my heart, my talents, and my service to Christ and his great cause. I want to so live for Christ each day that I may influence others to love and serve him. Oh, how I yearn for others to come with me that we may make our lives count for the Master.

SONG: "Take My Life, and Let It Be"

PRAYER

TAKE MY LIFE

Mrs. Maxine Morgan

(NOTE.—Prepare the responsive reading so that there will be a copy for each pupil. Make from poster board a large cross for the front of the room. On the cross have pinned or tacked enough small crosses for each person in the department to have one. If possible have the room lighted by candlelight and a spotlight on the cross. Play soft music as the pupils arrive. Just before the opening time have pianist play "Take My Life, and Let It Be.")

DUET: "Take My Life, and Let It Be"

SCRIPTURE READING: Matthew 16:21-27

RESPONSIVE READING (the superintendent will give the comments and the department will give the response):

Comment: Yes, deny himself, take up his cross and follow. Your cross may be the cross of temper. It is most difficult for you to control your temper; you like to answer back, you get angry easily. Bearing the cross of temper may be most difficult. Can you take up your cross and follow him?

Response: I will deny myself, take up my cross, and follow him.

Comment: Or perhaps your cross is that of envy or jealousy. Are you jealous of your friends when they have good fortune? Do you envy those who seem to have more money, more clothes, more popularity than you? Can you forget yourself and lose yourself in service to others? Can you take up your cross, if it is a cross of envy and jealousy?

169

Response: I will deny myself, take up my cross, and follow him.

Comment: Perhaps your cross will be inability to accomplish what you want in school and in life or perhaps it is a physical handicap. That cross will be a heavy one. Can you take up your cross and follow him by doing whatever it is your lot to do with enthusiasm, with patience and with perfectness? A fine woman having a decided limp, due to infantile paralysis when a child, cultivated the habit of smiling. Said she, "I want people to remember me, not by my limp but by my smile." She has made a most attractive personality and what a worker for her Lord. She is a typical ray of sunshine. Will you, too, take up your cross and follow him?

Response: I will deny myself, take up my cross, and follow him.

Comment: To take up your cross and follow Christ is not easy. We do not seek easy tasks if we are Christians. Taking up your cross may mean loss of friends, ridicule by family, changes in occupation —all difficult to endure. You know better than I what your cross is. Whatever it may be, will you take up that cross and follow Christ?

Response: I will deny myself, take up my cross and follow him.

Comment: You say that you will deny yourself, take up your cross, and follow him. If you mean that, then you are willing to put self completely in the background, to say, "Whatever my cross, I'll take it with thy help, O Christ," and follow no matter where, or when, or how. (Sing softly, "Wherever He Leads I'll Go.") Will you take up your cross and follow him?

Response: I will deny myself, take up my cross, and follow him.

Request (by the superintendent): As our pianist plays "Take My Life, and Let It Be," will you come forward and take one of these crosses for your own and return to your seat? (When the group has returned to their places with their crosses, sing " 'Are Ye Able,' Said the Master," first and fourth stanzas. Music continues softly.)

Conclusion (by the superintendent): Will you bow your heads and close your eyes? (Do not continue the program until every head is bowed and every eye closed.) If this morning you rededicate yourself to God, if you can say in your heart, "I will take up my cross and follow him to the best of my ability," then place your cross over your heart as we have our prayer.

Prayer (For the prayer, read the words of "Take My Life, and Let It Be" or the leader may give his own dedicatory prayer.)

MY LIFE FOR JESUS

Mrs. Henry Rogers

CHORUS (sung softly by a selected group): "I Am Thine, O Lord"

DUET: "My Prayer"

PRAYER: that God will use this program to bring about a greater consecration and the dedication of life to the Master

DISCUSSION (led by the superintendent): In Matthew 10:39 we find these words, "He that findeth his life shall lose it; and he that loseth his life for my sake shall find it." The verse just read points out the contrast between the selfish and the consecrated life. Those who live for self lose the joy of living, but those who consecrate their lives to him find abundant life. Do you recall any definite examples of this? (Voluntary response.)

This morning we are going to hear of others who have been willing to say as did Frances Havergal, "Take my life, and let it be Consecrated, Lord, to Thee." They found that the joys of life come from consecrated surrender to Christ.

(NOTE.—Show a flash card carrying the name of the one whose life is to be discussed. As the card with the name is flashed before the department, let the one who is to discuss this person begin talking immediately without announcement.)

STORY (by an Intermediate boy): "Paul"

172

One day a young man walked along a road leading to Damascus. As he traveled, he must have meditated on his mission. In the city just ahead lived many persons who called themselves Christians. They had dedicated their lives to Christ, and because they had this young man was determined that their lives be taken from them.

But something happened that day. The Saviour's voice spoke to this persecutor saying, "Saul, Saul, why persecutest thou me?" What was the result? (Response.) Yes, Saul surrendered his heart to Jesus and immediately dedicated his own life to Christianity's cause. The result? A changed individual and a blessing to the world who became not Saul the persecutor but Paul the beloved missionary who was able to write such words as these, "For to me to live is Christ, and to die is gain" (Phil. 1:21). No wonder people loved him during his lifetime and revere his name today. This is a reward of unselfish living.

Special Music (first stanza): "Jesus, I My Cross Have Taken"

Story (by a girl): "Mary Slessor"

In the long ago there lived a young Scottish girl named Mary Slessor. Very early in life she gave her heart to Christ and her life to God as a missionary.

One day she set sail for Africa and there until her death she found her life by losing it for Africa. Being a missionary in those days was often quite dangerous. Many of the Africans had never seen a white woman before. Their heathen practices were horrible, but Mary Slessor was absolutely unafraid. All alone she traveled into sections of Africa where no missionary had ever gone. (Chorus by concealed voices, "Just When I Need Him Most.") In spite of hardships, illness, and inconveniences she was privileged to lead hundreds to Christ. Her remains lie buried in that Dark Continent, but her memory lives on and on. Such a life can never die.

SPECIAL MUSIC (second stanza): "Jesus, I My Cross Have Taken"

STORY (by an Intermediate boy): "Just a Boy"

One summer a typical Intermediate boy made a great decision at a Baptist assembly. He had just graduated from high school. His trip to this meeting was a gift from interested friends. But in spite of the inspiration of the meeting, his heart was elsewhere for in his pocket he carried a signed contract for a vaudeville act. He had dramatic ability. A New York company recognizing this had given him a contract, and he planned to leave for further training soon after the assembly. The boy was elated. A glamorous career was ahead of him, and he was to begin work at one hundred dollars a week. His joy knew no bounds.

Many were attracted to the friendly, happy boy and were concerned over his choice for his life. One day some friends met and prayed for him for many hours. Later one of them said, "Tom, I hate to see you give your life to the devil instead of God." This set him to thinking and he became troubled. He was a Christian but was he giving his life to Satan? He prayed over it and at the closing consecration service he dedicated his life to God, threw aside his stage contract, and headed in a different direction.

Today he is a religious worker with young people, making much less salary even now than he was offered for the beginning of a stage career. But does he regret his decision? Let him answer. He says, "No indeed; I would do the same thing again. There is no happiness quite like that of dedicating one's life to God. It pays the biggest dividends of all."

SPECIAL MUSIC: "It Pays to Serve Jesus"

CONCLUSION (by the superintendent): How challenging are these examples of those who have given their lives to Christ. Perhaps you are saying, "Yes, and I want to dedicate my life to him but I do not know where he wants to use it." A beloved old minister says concerning this, "God opens and closes doors in revealing his plan to the young." Do well

175

each task that presents itself from day to day, then trust in God to reveal his work to you. He will always lead those who are willing to follow his guidance. (More advice along this line may be given if time permits. A simple vocational guidance outline may be placed on the blackboard.)

If you are willing to dedicate your life to Christ and to trust his guidance for your life's work, will you stand and sing with our soloist the first stanza of "Jesus, I My Cross Have Taken"?

PRAYER

MISSIONS

BAPTIST MISSIONS IN MY STATE

Ina S. Lambdin

PIANO MEDITATION: "Send the Light"

SCRIPTURE READING (by the girls): Proverbs 14: 34

PRAYER (by boys): that our state may be aggressive in its fight against sin

MAP TALK (by an older Intermediate): "Some Religious Needs of My State"

(NOTE.—Place a large map of the state at the front of the room. Using not more than two minutes, an older Intermediate may sketch briefly the religious condition of the state—number of unsaved people, number who do not attend church, and any other striking facts. He can consult the minutes of his Baptist state convention and his pastor for these facts.)

SONG (written on blackboard and sung to the tune of "America"): "My State"

> My state, my home, my pride!
> In all the world beside,
> No spot more fair.
> May God whose name we praise
> Direct thee in thy ways,
> Through all the coming days
> This is my prayer.

PLAYLET

SCENE: *Office of state mission secretary. Some of the state mission workers have gathered for a conference about their work.*

179

STATE MISSION SECRETARY: Your letters about your work this month have thrilled my soul. I am eager for each of you to tell the others about what you are doing. I'm sorry all our workers couldn't be present to rejoice with us, but they had duties elsewhere. I'll try to give you a few interesting things about their work. As your leader, I've visited more churches this month than I've been able to reach any month since I became your secretary. Everywhere the people seem to be waking up to religious needs in our state and realizing that each church and each individual must help. Our collections for the entire program have been most encouraging. Mr. ―― (state Sunday school secretary), give us some high lights in your work of the month.

STATE SUNDAY SCHOOL SECRETARY: I hardly know where to begin. Your department workers and I organized two Sunday schools this month and we helped to put new life into two others. We had an enlargement campaign in one country church which needed repairing very badly. Before the end of the week, enthusiasm ran so high that the men volunteered to repair the church, paint it, and start all over. It was a glorious experience.

STATE MISSION SECRETARY: Thank you, Mr. ――. We rejoice with you. I am sorry Mr. ――, our Baptist Training Union secretary, couldn't be here but he has been hard at work. In addition to his regular routine of organizing new Unions, teaching study courses, and helping the young people generally, he has sponsored a movement to help prevent repeal of our state prohibition laws. In one city he organized a parade that was so big it looked as if the whole population had turned out. Our state was kept in the dry column and we rejoice that one of our state mission workers had such a big part in upholding the cause of righteousness in our state. Mr. —— (superintendent of orphanage), how is our orphanage getting along?

SUPERINTENDENT OF ORPHANAGE: The best ever! Only we need more room. We have more children than we can take care of and dozens are begging to come. Won't all of you tell the people of the state more about our needs as you go around?

W.M.U. SECRETARY: The women of the state are doing all they can to help our orphans, Mr. ——. As the rest of you talked I could hardly wait for my time. This last week I organized a W.M.S. in a church which had not given one cent to missions in the history of the church. I believe they've caught a vision of how they may help give Christ to our state and to the world. We've had more mission study classes reported this month than any month this year.

181

STATE MISSION SECRETARY: Thank you. Now we want a word from Brother Black, one of our heroic missionary pastors.

BROTHER BLACK: First, I want to express my appreciation again for the help the State Mission Board has given my church and many others like it which are not financially able to pay their pastors a living salary. My church is in a mill section, but the opportunities to witness for Christ are unlimited. Most of the people have had no religious advantages. We have just closed a revival where twenty-five were saved.

STATE MISSION SECRETARY: My heart rejoices in these reports and I know yours do. I am sorry that representatives of our Baptist schools and hospital couldn't be here today. They are greatly in need of funds but they are carrying on in a fine way. We are looking forward to the day when every Baptist in our state will be so interested in giving the gospel to those around us that no appeals for funds will have to be made. Every one will give because he loves his neighbor and his God. Let's go back to our tasks with new enthusiasm and do our best to arouse our people and help each one to feel his responsibility for bringing in the kingdom in our state.

PRAYER (Ask God to help every Intermediate to make a sacrificial gift for missions in his own state.)

(NOTE.—Adapt this program to present needs in your state.)

HOME MISSIONS IN COLORS

Mrs. Myrtle Creasman

(Note.—Place flags about the front of the assembly room.)

Soft Music: "America the Beautiful"

Song: "America the Beautiful"

Discussion (by the superintendent): We are directing our thoughts today to the part of America in which we live—our Southland. Our Scripture lesson is Moses' description of the Land of Canaan. As this is read, let us notice how well it can be used as a description of our Southland.

Scripture Reading (read by the department): Deuteronomy 8:6-10

Poem (by a teacher): "There Is No Land Like Ours"

> Though other lands may proudly boast
> Of castles, moats and towers,
> Of charms our country has the most
> There is no land like ours.
>
> Though other lands may proudly tell
> Of rarest fruits and flowers
> For nature's charms on hill, in dell
> There is no land like ours.
>
> Though other lands with tales entrance
> Of lovely nooks and bowers
> For history's lore and real romance
> There is no land like ours.

Hail to the south, the wonderland
Which God so richly dowers!
From east to west, from strand to strand,
There is no land like ours.

—MRS. MYRTLE CREASMAN

PRAYER: thanking God for the privilege of living in the Southland

PRESENTATION (by the superintendent): "Home Missions in Colors"

We would enjoy thinking of our Southland in the colors her natural beauty provides—her amber fields of grain, her purple majesties, her blue skies, her green trees, her flowers of a thousand hues. But since this is a home mission program we must turn our color thoughts into another channel as we use different colors to represent different races of people living in the South.

(NOTE.—On six sheets of construction paper print names of home mission groups as follows: on a red sheet, Indians; on a black sheet, Negroes; on a purple sheet, Jews; on a blue sheet, French; on a yellow sheet, foreigners; and on a white sheet, mountaineers, deaf mutes, others. As the superintendent speaks he holds up the color about which he is talking.)

1. *Red.*—First, we think of the red race. These should be first in our consideration because they were the first Americans. We are indebted to them for the wonderful land in which we live, and the best way to pay this debt is to tell them about Jesus. This we are doing through our home missionaries who work among small groups of Indians in Florida, Alabama, and North Carolina, and among the larger

184

groups who live on reservations in Oklahoma, New Mexico, and Arizona. Through this work many Indians have left the pagan ways of the red race to walk in the Jesus way.

2. *Black.*—A large per cent of the population of the South belongs to the black race. While many Negroes are Christians, millions are still unevangelized. Our Home Mission Board provides teacher-missionaries who, by working in Negro colleges, holding institutes for Negro ministers, and by other methods, are training Negro leaders who shall evangelize their own people.

3. *Purple.*—The royal purple is a fitting color to represent the Jews, the people of the King of kings. Of the half million Jews living in the South only a scattered few are Christians. Jacob Gartenhaus, a converted Jew, is our home missionary among his own people. His ministry is twofold. He tries to contact the Jews themselves that he may win them to Christ; and he seeks to enlist Southern Baptists that they may be missionaries to their Jewish neighbors. He says that Jews are more responsive to the gospel than ever before, and that many of them are accepting Jesus as their Messiah.

4. *Blue.*—We are using the lovely blue color to represent the French people of Louisiana. Since blue stands for truth, it might also suggest their great need of the truth of God's Word. These have

been citizens of our nation for many generations, but they live to themselves, not speaking our language and knowing little about American life. Many of them grown to manhood and womanhood have never heard of the Constitution of the United States and have never seen a Bible. Our home missionaries are carrying the gospel message to them and many of them are being won to Christ. In our home mission school, Acadia Academy, French leaders are being trained.

5. *Yellow.*—We shall let the yellow stand for those of many races in the South. Some, the Chinese really belong to the yellow race, but we are including in this group the Mexicans, Italians, Cubans, and all other foreign people. Our largest group of home missionaries work among the Mexicans of the Southwest. We also have missionaries among the Italians in Tampa, Florida; Ensley, Alabama; and Kansas City, Missouri; among the Cubans in Tampa; the Chinese in Norfolk, Virginia; San Antonio, Texas; El Paso, Texas; and Phoenix, Arizona; while in the industrial area of East St. Louis, Illinois, and in other centers of foreign population, our missionaries minister to those speaking twenty-six different languages.

6. *White.*—We are using this white sheet to represent several home mission groups who belong to the white race. The mountaineers constitute per-

haps the purest Anglo-Saxon stock to be found among our Southern population. Our home missionaries work organizing Sunday school classes and in other ways trying to reach them with the gospel. Then there are other neglected groups in the congested cities and in the country sections to whom we, through our Home Mission Board, are sending missionaries.

CONCLUSION: We have had this colorful view of our home mission work. This has helped us realize how many races of people we have living in our own land, and how needful they are of the gospel. How fine if each of you will take as a special object of prayer one of these particular groups; also what a blessing if you would give a special love gift for home missions.

PRAYER:

> Lord! while for all mankind we pray,
>   Of every clime and coast,
> O hear us for our native land,—
>   The land we love the most.
>
> Lord of the nations! thus to thee
>   Our country we commend;
> Be thou her refuge and her trust,
>   Her everlasting friend.
>
> —JOHN WERFORD

HANDING ON THE LIGHT

Lizzie Waite

(NOTE.—Give each person a small birthday candle as he enters. If possible, have the program typed or mimeographed and give each a copy. Place a tall, white candle in the center of the table at the front of the assembly room. On each side of this place six candle holders. Select a teacher or officer to read all the Scripture references. He should stand to one side at the front of the room, and be seated after each reference.)

CALL TO WORSHIP: "Jesus Shall Reign"

PRAYER

SONG (first and fourth stanzas): "Jesus Saves"

SCRIPTURE READING: "The Coming of the Light of Jesus"—John 1:1-10

PIANO SOLO: "Joy to the World"

(NOTE.—While this song is being played, a girl enters very slowly from the hall with a lighted taper and lights the candle in the center of the table. As the candle is being lighted, the reader quotes John 8:12.)

SONG (first stanza and chorus): "The Light of the World Is Jesus"

(NOTE.—The department will sing all the lines except, "The Light of the World Is Jesus"; these lines are to be sung each time by soloist.)

SCRIPTURE READING: "Handing on the Light to the Disciples," John 12:35-36; Matthew 5:15-16.

(NOTE.—Ask twelve boys to sit at the front and give each an unlighted candle—smaller than the one on the table.)

SONG: "Hail to the Brightness"

(NOTE.—As this song is sung each of the twelve boys, one at a time and each waiting until the other is seated, goes to the table and lights his candle from the tall white one and places it in one of the holders.)

SCRIPTURE READING: "The Light Shed Abroad," Acts 1:6b-8

MISSIONS

(NOTE.—This program is adapted from one which appeared in the *Homiletic Review*, February 1933, p. 120.)

SONG (first stanza): "We've a Story to Tell to the Nations"

(NOTE.—During the singing of this song, two girls carrying yellow tapers, enter at the same time from different sides of the room, and light their candles from one of the twelve on the table. After lighting them, one girl stands at the right side and the other at the left side of the table holding their candles.)

SCRIPTURE READING: "The Light Through Missions," Matthew 28:19-20

SONG: "O Zion, Haste"

(NOTE.—During the singing of this hymn, four boys and girls dressed to represent different nations, come from four parts of the room carrying green candles. They go to the two girls holding the yellow candles and light theirs. Then each speaks briefly of the mission work and needs of the country he represents [see mission journals] after which each of the four goes back to the classroom from which he has come, and stands in the door holding the lighted candles, remaining there during the rest of the program.)

SCRIPTURE READING: "Walking in the Light," 1 John 1:6-7

SONG (first and second stanzas): "Send the Light"

(NOTE.—While the department is singing this song, the two girls standing in the front of the room pass down the aisles and light the candles of those sitting next to them, and so on down the rows until everybody in the room is holding a lighted candle.)

SOLO: "Wherever He Leads I'll Go"

PRAYER: that each of us may do our part in helping to send the light to the ends of the earth; that we will covenant with God to do more than we have ever done before

SPECIAL DAYS

TAKING INVENTORY
(New Year)

Lula Bell Crenshaw

CALL TO WORSHIP: "My Desire"

CHORUS: "My Desire"

SOLO (Concealed soloist; department sings the chorus): "It Pays to Serve Jesus"

PRAYER

DISCUSSION (led by the superintendent). How quickly the past year has slipped by and now that we are launching a new year, suppose we take an inventory! Webster says that "inventory" is an itemized list of goods, with their estimated worth, so we want to look into our storehouse of life this morning and see what worthy *qualities* we have stored up the past year and what we shall put into *this new year*. Of course, we must consider the cost, since everything of value costs *something*. Let us list on the blackboard only the valuable qualities we find with their worth and cost.

(NOTE.—If the program could be mimeographed and a copy given to each one present, it would be well worth while.)

We will ask the teachers to help us search the shelves of the storehouse and tell us what valuable goods we have there, and you may tell something of its cost and of what worth it is to you.

(NOTE.—Teachers should be told beforehand to suggest the following qualities. Pause after each quality is suggested and give pupils opportunity to state what the value of each is to their lives, also the cost. Write suggestions on the blackboard, making whatever comments or applications are necessary or desired. The following are only suggestive.)

Courage (by a teacher): Joshua 1:9

Value

1. Gives strength to resist temptation
2. Develops ability to do
3. Takes away timidity
4. Increases self-confidence

Cost

1. Doing the hard and difficult things
2. Refusing to give in to fear of self, others or things

Purity (by a teacher): Matthew 5:8

Value

1. Increases self-respect
2. Leads to genuine friendships
3. Strengthens respect of others
4. Makes a real dwelling place in the heart for God

Cost

1. Giving up the crowd
2. Loneliness or loss of some friendships
3. Becoming a target for sarcasm and raillery
4. Denying self of petty pleasures

Kindness (by a teacher): Ephesians 4:32

Value

1. Makes for happiness
2. Develops graciousness
3. Attracts friends
4. Influences for Christ

Cost

1. Restrains from sarcasms, hurtful criticisms, ridicule, spite, and other undesirable traits
2. Thinks of others first

Faith (by a teacher): Hebrews 11:6

Value

1. Shields against temptation
2. Eliminates fear
3. Develops self-confidence
4. Gives power
5. Pleases God

Cost

1. Following Christ through hardships
2. Being cheerful and smiling
3. Always expecting the best
4. Exerting a "can" rather than a "can't" attitude

Honesty (by a teacher): Romans 12:17

Value

1. Gives self-respect
2. Merits respect of others
3. Clears conscience

Cost

1. Often calls for sacrifice of worldly possessions
2. Sometimes means losing the game

Unselfishness (by a teacher): 1 Corinthians 10:32-33

Value

1. Contributes deep and genuine joy
2. Increases growth in spirituality
3. Wins love of friends and others

Cost

1. Putting Christ first
2. Putting others before self
3. Giving up comforts, conveniences and the like
4. Sacrificing personal desires

Christlikeness (by a teacher): John 13:15

Value

1. Makes for fruitful lives
2. Gives security
3. Increases drawing power
4. Assures real happiness

Cost

1. Spending much time in Bible reading and prayer
2. Giving of self
3. Loving the unlovely
4. Serving others daily

Conclusion (by the superintendent): There are other valuable possessions in our storehouse that we will not have time to mention this morning, but the question for our hearts is, Has each of us all of these qualities in our individual storehouse? or have courage and faith been destroyed by temptations yielded to and by fear and lack of self-confidence? Has purity been soiled by foul words and thoughts and by too intimate contacts with others of the "crowd"? Or, has honesty been tarnished by just a little cheating somewhere; while kindness and unselfishness have been consumed in the desire for self-glory and conceit?

As you begin a new year will you covenant with God to endeavor to grow more Christlike? To make your life more fruitful? To resist temptation? To have an abiding joy, greater respect, a growing consciousness of God's presence? Will you do your best to practice his presence throughout this year?

Scripture Reading (read by a good reader): 2 Peter 1:2-9

Song: "My Desire"

THE NEW LIFE

(Easter)

Mrs. Elbert Hardin

(NOTE.—Place a bowl of lilies at the front of the assembly room near a picture of Sallman's, *The Son of Man.*)

MEDITATION (orchestra if possible, or violin): "Were You There When They Crucified My Lord?"

POEM (unannounced and read by one who has a good voice and will interpret the full meaning):

It happened on an April day,
　　Bounded by skies so blue and still,
And olive trees all hushed and gray,
　　They led one up a skull-shaped hill
Followed by a crowd whose piercing cry
　　Was, "Crucify!"

It happened on an April morn,
　　They nailed a man upon a tree
Whose head was circled with sharp thorn,
　　Lifted Him high that all might see
His angony, His heaving breath,
　　His awful death.

It happened on an April eve—
　　The air was cut by one sharp cry
That wine nor gall could not relieve
　　"Eli—lama—Sabachthani!"
Then lightning, thunder crack on crack,
　　The sun was black.

198

It happened on an April day
    They tombed a Man (the crowd had fled,
Sealed it; and set a watch that way
    To flout His words; to prove Him dead;
And show Himself he could not save
    From the dark grave.

It happened on an April day . . .
    A tremor shook the paling gloom,
A white flame tore the door away,
    Life came a victor from the tomb,
Love cannot die, nor truth betray . . .
    Christ rose upon an April day!

—JOHN RICHARD MORELAND

—From *Christ and the Fine Arts*, Maus, pp. 444-445. Published by Harper Brothers. Used by special permission.

SILENT PRAYER: a prayer of thanks for Christ who arose and lives today

TALK (by the superintendent): What does Easter mean to you? Does it just mean that spring has come after the long winter? Does it mean birds singing? Flowers blooming? Budding trees? Sweet odors? New life everywhere? Does it mean coming to church? Going reverently into God's house? Listening to beautiful music? Seeing the white lilies in their setting of green? Does it mean all this outward beauty and form of worship? In the midst of the sanctuary do we see the bright new bonnets and beautiful dresses of those who chose this day to show gladness by their raiment?

199

Certainly we think of all these things, but unless there is more, we might be heathen people, worshiping the goddess of spring or beauty.

We sing, "Christ the Lord Is Risen Today," and we observe this day in commemoration of his resurrection.

What did it mean that first Easter morning? The darkest night ever known to man descended upon the earth. The beloved Christ had suffered shameful death. He had been buried in a tomb hewn out of rock, and a huge stone had been placed across the door. The Roman seal was stamped upon it and guards set to watch it. Hope was dead. The disciples were stunned, bewildered, sick at heart. Then, with the dawn of Sunday, an earthquake came. Angels rolled back the stone. The Son of God came forth from the tomb which could not hold him. Guards fell as if dead. To those first loved ones who came to the tomb to minister to their Lord, the angels said, "He is not here: for he is risen . . . go quickly and tell his disciples."

Could such a wondrous thing be true? They came and saw the empty tomb and heard the angels say again, "He is risen as he said." The Lord himself appeared to Mary Magdalene as she wept. Slowly the glorious truth forced itself upon them, until as they were gathered behind closed doors in the evening, Jesus appeared in their midst and showed them his pierced hands and side that they might indeed know he was the risen Lord.

Not only did he show himself to them there, but he showed himself many times during the forty days he stayed on earth before he ascended to heaven. Hundreds of people saw him. It is a historical fact beyond dispute that he arose from the grave. But it is more than history. Some of our girls will tell us what it means:

(NOTE.—Assign the following four parts at least one week in advance. Ask pupils to read the Scripture references and comment on them.)

1. It means that because Christ conquered death we too may live again after we die. 1 Corinthians 15:21-22; John 11:25-26.

2. It means that Christ is our living Lord today and will help and understand us better than our closest earthly friend. John 15:4-5, 9-10.

3. It means that we may have a home in heaven, and see and know our loved ones who have gone on before. John 14:2-3; Hebrews 11:10, 16.

4. Because Christ conquered death he also conquered sin, sorrow, suffering, and all other evils. Through him, we can also conquer. John 16:33; 1 Corinthians 15:26, 56-57.

SONG: "Christ Arose"

PRAYER: that daily we may be more conscious of our living Lord, and that those who do not know him may turn to him today

MOTHER'S DAY

Elizabeth Wray

(NOTE.—Plan to have the mothers of the boys and girls as guests. Pin a red or white flower on each.)

PRELUDE: "Home, Sweet Home"

CALL TO WORSHIP (led by the superintendent): "Honour thy father and thy mother: that thy days may be long upon the land which the Lord thy God giveth thee" (Ex. 20:12).

RESPONSE (by department): For God commanded, saying, "Honour thy father and mother: and, He that curseth father or mother, let him die the death" (Matt. 15:4).

SONG: "Mother's Doxology"

> Praise God for mother, home and love;
> Praise Him for Bible from above;
> Praise Him for church and country dear;
> Praise Him for Christ throughout the year.
> —NEVADA MILLER WHITWELL, in *Intermediate Expressional Services*

PRAYER

SOLO: "Mothers" (Tune: "Beautiful Dreams")

> Let's join together, happy and gay,
> Praising our mothers on this holy day.
> Lessons they've taught us, how we should live,
> With love and kindness, and freely to give.
> Mother, my dearest, gentle and brave,
> Many the kisses and smiles that you gave
> To cheer and help me along my way—
> To cheer and help me along my way.
> Mother, my dearest, I praise you today.

202

Christ's mother, Mary, gentle and sweet,
Cared for our Saviour and wept at his feet,
Showing that mother's devotion is true,
In joy and sorrow all our life through.
Giving us hope by patience and love
Guided by power from Heaven above.
Let the world listen, let praises ring
Songs to all mothers so gladly we sing
Songs to all mothers so gladly we sing.

—ALICE REED. *Used by permission.*

SONG: "Oh, Mother Dear" (Tune: America the Beautiful)

Oh, beautiful this Mother's Day,
  On which we give you praise;
To you who've watched and guided us
  Through all our childish days.
Oh, mother dear, you were so kind,
  So good, so sweet, so true,
That we shall try our very best
  To praise and honor you.

Oh, beautiful the love of God,
  Who sent His Son on earth;
Oh, beautiful that mother mild
  Who gave our dear Lord birth.
Oh, mother dear, we sing to you
  Upon this happy day,
And may you live to guide our steps
  Along life's rugged way.

—NEVADA MILLER WHITWELL, in
Intermediate Worship Service.
Used by permission.

SCRIPTURE: Proverbs 31:10-15, 19-23, 25-31

COMMENTS (by the superintendent): Every day in the year we should honor our mothers. However, the idea of one special day being set aside as "Mother's Day" originated with Miss Anna Jarvis of Philadelphia in 1908 when she assisted in a memorial service at the church in a small Virginia town where her mother had been an active member. Through Miss Jarvis' influence, some years later Congress suggested to the President that a day be set apart on which to honor mothers. President Wilson approved the plan, and on May 9, 1914, issued a proclamation ordering the flag to be displayed in all government buildings and urging the people to display flags at their homes on the second Sunday in May, as a public expression of respect for the mothers of our country. And so it has now become a universal custom in our country to honor mothers on the second Sunday in May.

RESPONSE

1. "If I had all the mothers I ever saw to choose from, I would have chosen you."

—CARLYLE

2. "Mother! Her love and mindfulness have never failed me. I am as sure to have them as I am to have the sunshine, air to breathe, or God's mercy."

—FRANCES E. WILLARD

3. "The love of mother never changes, never tires; in good or bad repute; in the face of the world's frowns, mother's love lives on."

—WASHINGTON IRVING

4. "The greatest possession which can bless and sanctify a boy's life is the memory of a praying Christian mother."

—J. A. GARFIELD

5. "I am more indebted to my mother than to all others except my God."

—MARY LYON

SOLO: "That Wonderful Mother of Mine"

POEM: "Mother Mine"

> You loved when I was but a child,
>   Rocked me when I was ill;
> You always were so comforting
>   When leading up life's hill.
> And when at night, beside my bed,
>   I kneeled and there my prayer was said,
> My hand and yours were closed entwined;
>   Your love has always 'round me shined—
> God bless you, Mother, Mother mine.
>
> You worked that I might stay in school,
>   You soothed away my fears;
> Oft when I came at eventime
>   Your cheek was wet with tears.
> And when the shadows lengthened,
>   I came to you to hear
> A word of gentle sympathy
>   To charm away my fears.

You told me of a Father
  Who knoweth and who cares;
God bless you, Mother darling!
  You're the heart of all my prayers.
And when, some day I reach the home
  Of all the saints divine,
I'll say I'm here because God gave
  That precious Mother mine.

PRAYER: gratitude for our mothers

SONG: "Faith of Our Mothers" (Tune: "Faith of Our Fathers")

Faith of our mothers, living still,
  Which she to us, her children gave,
Through storm and sunshine, heat and chill,
  Lives on to bless, our souls to save.
Faith of our mothers, living faith,
  We will be true to thee till death.

Faith of our mothers, living still
  In hearts of sons, and daughters true,
They rally now to fight for thee;
  Strong they to bear and strong to do,
Faith of our mothers, saving faith,
  We will be true to thee till death.

(NOTE.—"Mother's Doxology" is taken from *Intermediate Expressional Service*, by Nevada Miller Whitwell. "Oh, Mother Dear," "Mother Mine," and "Faith of Our Mothers," are taken from *Intermediate Worship Service*, by Whitwell. Standard Publishing Company. Used by permission.)

MEMORIAL DAY

Mary Alice Biby

PLAYLET

(NOTE.—Arrange the front of the department as a living room. Put the piano at a cozy angle. Place rockers, a table, flowers, magazines, and attractive, colorful pillows about the room. Make this a conversational program given by several seated about the room. Ask that they assume a listening attitude as "America the Beautiful," is sung by the department.)

HELEN (at the close of the first stanza): How I do appreciate that song! Let's pause right here and thank God for our country, for those who fought for it and made it free. (Offers a prayer. At the close of the prayer all remain with bowed heads as second verse of the same song is sung, this being followed by a prayer thanking God for the Pilgrims who braved so much for religious freedom.)

DUET: "Faith of Our Fathers"

JAMES: Do you know I have not heard that old, old poem about the Pilgrims for so long. Mary, suppose you quote it for us. Let's all notice particularly the last two verses.

MARY: I, too, like that poem and shall be glad to quote it. ("The Landing of the Pilgrim Fathers" as pianist plays real softly, "America the Beautiful.")

At the close of the poem all join in singing last two verses of, "America the Beautiful."

207

Landing of the Pilgrim Fathers

The breaking waves dashed high
  On a stern and rock-bound coast,
And the woods against a stormy sky
  Their giant branches tossed;

And the heavy night hung dark
  The hills and waters o'er,
When a band of exiles moored their bark
  On the wild New England shore.

Not as the conqueror comes,
  They, the true hearted, came;
Not with the roll of the stirring drums,
  And the trumpet that sings of fame;

Not as the flying come,
  In silence and in fear;
They shook the depths of the desert gloom
  With their hymns of lofty cheer.

Amid the storm they sang,
  And the stars heard, and the sea,
And the sounding aisles of the dim woods rang
  To the anthem of the free.

The ocean eagle soared
  From his nest by the white wave's foam;
And the rocking pines of the forest roared,—
  This was their welcome home.

There were men with hoary hair
  Amid that pilgrim band:—
Why had they come to wither there,
  Away from their childhood's land?

There was woman's fearless eye,
    Lit by her deep love's truth;
There was manhood's brow, serenely high,
    And the fiery heart of youth.

What sought they thus afar?
    Bright jewels of the mine,
The weather of seas, the spoils of war?
    They sought a faith's pure shrine.

Ay, call it holy ground,
    The spot where first they trod;
They have left unstained what there they found—
    Freedom to worship God.
                    —FELICIA D. HEMANS

WILLIAM: This old country of ours has seen some rather severe strife in its efforts to keep itself a country of which its citizens may well be proud.

WILMA: Yes, indeed, what suffering and what battles! Take the Revolutionary War for example. How our countrymen did show their true worth. Heroes indeed! What a joy to honor them. (Here several of the outstanding heroes of that war with a brief comment may be mentioned by different ones in a conversational manner.)

FRANCES: Then too, the Civil War called forth wonderful and mighty heroes of faith and pride. (Different ones mention and tell briefly of several. If desired during these comments the pianist may play softly, "America the Beautiful.")

JOHN: Let us again bow our heads as we thank God for these great men.

JANET: And, then how very proud of her sons and daughters was our country during both of the world wars. (Brief talk on these.)

WILLIAM: Surely, when so much has been done to give us a nation of religious and other freedom along with high ideals we ought to do our part by striving to prove citizens in which our country may take pride. Shall we not consecrate our lives, spend more time in prayer and the study of his Word and in actual service for him that we may really prove worthy of the great sacrifice made in order that America may be a nation accepted unto God.

(NOTE.—All stand as one enters with a large American flag. As the one bearing the flag comes to the front of the platform all unite in singing first and last stanzas of "America." As the last stanza is being sung a girl enters with the Christian flag and stands by the one bearing the American flag. At the close of the song a concealed soloist sings softly, "God Bless America" as the department stands with bowed heads.)

PRAYER: for sick and disabled soldiers and for loved ones of those who have fallen in battle

FATHER'S DAY

Clara Mae Macke

(NOTE.—It would mean much to have the fathers as guests. If this is done arrange to give a boutonniere to each one. Appoint girls to pin these on as fathers arrive. Be sure to give special recognition to these fathers.)

CALL TO WORSHIP: "Into My Heart"

CHORUS (Sung softly with bowed heads): "Into My Heart"

SONG (first and last stanzas): "Faith of Our Fathers"

DISCUSSION (by the superintendent): Our program is given in honor of our fathers. "Mrs. John Bruce Dodd launched a movement in her home town, Spokane, Washington, as a tribute to her father, William J. Smart, who reared his motherless children alone. In 1910 Mrs. Dodd drew up a petition and addressed it to the Ministerial Association of Spokane, urging constructive teaching from the pulpit—teaching that would point out the father's rightful place in the home. The newspapers helped to launch the movement, but did not take it very seriously, 'intimating that father's business was to pay the bills and crank the Ford.' Misunderstanding about the date arose, but at last the third Sunday in June was accepted. Red and white roses were suggested as the symbol or flower for this day. A red rose for the living father and the white rose for the father who has passed to his reward."

POEM: *Only a Dad*

Only a dad with a tired face,
Coming home from the daily race,
Bringing the little of gold or fame
To show how well he has played the game,

But glad in his heart that his own rejoice
To see him come and hear his voice
Only a dad with a brood of four,
One of ten million men or more,

Plodding along in the daily strife,
Bearing the whips and scorns of life
With never a whimper of pain or hate
For the sake of those who at home await.

Only a dad, neither rich or proud,
Merely one of the surging crowd,
Toiling, striving from day to day,
Facing whatever may come his way,

Silent whenever the harsh condemn
And bearing it all for the life of them.
Only a dad, but he gave his all
To smooth the way for his children small

Doing, with courage stern and grim,
The deeds that his father did for him,
This is the line that for him I pen,
Only a dad, but the best of men.

This poem is from the COLLECTED
VERSE OF EDGAR A. GUEST, copyright 1945. Used by permission
of The Reilly and Lee Co.,
Chicago.

STUDYING FATHERS OF THE BIBLE (led by the superintendent): I want you to think of the names of some good fathers that are mentioned in the Bible. (As the names are mentioned, ask a boy to list them on the blackboard. Ask the pupils to mention at least one son of each man listed. Have these written opposite the father's name.)

All of these sons had very noble fathers, and most of the fathers whose names are listed on the board had fine Christian sons.

At this time we are going to think of the finest, cleanest, and only perfect Son who ever lived. Can you name him? Yes, it is Jesus. We know what an obedient Son Jesus was. He always did the will of his father. Remember how in Gethsemane, when the burden of your sins and my sins was so heavy that he cried, "Father if it be possible, let this cup pass from me." Then, how in submission to his father's will, he prayed, "Nevertheless, not as I will, but as thou wilt."

Suppose we hear what Jesus had to say about his Father.

SCRIPTURE READING (by individual pupils. Paste seals of Christ on plain calling cards and write one of these references on each, giving cards out before the program begins and asking each pupil to stand and read his reference when called for): John 10:30;

Luke 2:49; John 5:17; John 14:28; John 16:27; Psalm 103:13; Matthew 15:4; Matthew 10:37.

(NOTE.—By department in unison): 2 Corinthians 6:17-18

CONCLUSION (by the superintendent): We prove our love to our earthly fathers by obeying them and doing what we can to make them happy. They have sacrificed for us and have given us their best. If reverence and obedience is due them, how much more do we owe our Heavenly Father, who loves us so much that he gave us his best—his only Son. How can Intermediates ever repay him for his great sacrifice? There is only one way—that is to surrender your lives unreservedly to him.

SOLO: "Satisfied with Jesus"

PRAYER

WHERE SHALL I GO TO COLLEGE?

Grace Dryden Spindle

(NOTE.—Work for a college atmosphere. Arrange pennants from various schools on the walls. Display a number of school catalogues. Ask several boys and girls in school attire to sit and stand at the front of the assembly room as they ask questions of a college graduate. Questions may be: What good does a college education do? What should determine the selection of a college? How early ought I decide about what I'm going to be? As they talk the pianist begins playing.)

SOFT MUSIC: "Our Best"

SCRIPTURE READING (read by the department): "Peter's Recipe for Doing Our Best" 2 Peter 1:2-8

DISCUSSION (led by the superintendent): How I appreciate the interest you boys and girls are showing in a college education. Of course, you can do much without college but I feel that you can do so much more in the same length of time with college background and training. In recent years we have been hearing a great deal about a "balanced diet." We have become "vitamin conscious" as we have been brought to realize that certain vitamins or elements present in foods are necessary for our physical well being. Scientists, dietitians, and doctors tell us that harmful effects can come as a result of an improper, unbalanced diet, and we all know how much more susceptible to diseases of all kinds are those persons who have been physically undernourished.

The word educate comes from a Latin word meaning "to nourish" or "to develop." And just as we need a balanced diet in the food we eat, so in our educational process do we need to be nourished and developed in a completely balanced diet. God has so wonderfully and completely made man that each one of us possesses a fourfold nature—a physical, mental, moral, and spiritual nature. Each of these must be developed and nourished if our lives are to be well rounded and complete. Therefore, any school that trains only our mental and physical natures and leaves the moral and spiritual undeveloped is offering us an unbalanced diet. I am sure we do not want our moral and spiritual natures to go under-nourished.

SCRIPTURE READING (read in unison as you lead the pupils to see the completeness of Jesus' development): Luke 2:52

TALK (by the superintendent): "Baptist Schools"

Southern Baptists, through the Co-operative Program and through gifts of generous hearted Christian men and women, are supporting and maintaining numbers of schools including senior colleges, junior colleges, academies, a woman's training school, two theological schools, and one Bible institute. These schools offer the greatest opportunity for Christian training in a Christian atmosphere and for the complete development of the whole being—physical, mental, moral, and spiritual.

In our own state there are (give number) of these Baptist schools. Who can name these and tell where they are located? (Voluntary response.)

(Note.—It would be splendid if a map of your state on which your various schools and colleges are located could be placed before the department. Write your state Sunday school secretary for this information.)

Talk (by a teacher of boys): "Baptist School Advantages"

I am sure that many of you are asking in your hearts, "Of what advantage can it be to me to go to one of these Baptist schools?" I am giving some reasons—

1. Our Baptist schools are small. This presents the decided advantage of closer personal contact with the students and teachers in all the activities of the school. You will have a better opportunity "to make yourself count"; you will not be submerged in a great mass of students.

2. In our Baptist schools you will have ample opportunity to develop leadership in all phases of school life—scholastic, athletic, social, and religious. Your spiritual development will not be neglected. The Bible and the chapel services will be magnified.

3. The professors and other instructors being Christians seek to build up—not tear down American citizenship.

4. Fellow students will be boys and girls who are trying to develop into useful, trained Christian citi-

zens. Your character and conduct will be greatly influenced by these associates during this period of your life.

SONG: "A Charge to Keep"

TALK (by a teacher of girls): "Today's Need for Christian Education"

Although most of our Baptist schools are small, they have high standards of scholarship; they offer splendid courses of instruction; they employ high-type Christian teachers. Every year they help provide our country with Christian doctors and scientists, Christian lawyers and judges, Christian businessmen and merchants, Christian teachers, professors, and college presidents, Christian farmers and Christian men and women in all walks of life. Our country is in great need of such men and women for frank, fearless, intelligent Christian leadership.

A Southern girl, greatly distressed at the appalling conditions she found in the so-called society schools which she was attending, wrote home: "Mother, only one of my professors is a real American; the rest are all Communists." And in a distant state the newly elected president of a state-controlled college was exceedingly disturbed to learn that although the professors in that school very ably taught their chosen subjects in the classroom, on the campus many of them spread an insidious propaganda that our government should be overthrown and destroyed. Viewing such alarming conditions as these, we readily agree with Roger Babson when he says, "The safety of our nation, including all groups, depends upon Christian education."

CONCLUSION (by the superintendent): A number of you boys and girls are already thinking about what you shall be in life and, of course, you are thinking about going to college. It will be fine if you can decide definitely what you are going to be before starting your college work for then you can select the subjects which will be most helpful. I wonder how many of you have decided just which college you will attend (show of hands). I hope you will pray much and seek God's guidance in this matter, for it is such an important decision—one which will affect your whole life. May God lead you to choose a Christian school supported by our Baptist people.

PRAYER: for God's guidance in this important decision

MY ATTITUDE TOWARD DRINKING

C. Aubrey Hearn

(NOTE.—See the book, *Alcohol the Destroyer*, Hearn, pages 142-156, for suggestions in creating atmosphere for this program.)

MEDITATION: "Yield Not to Temptation"

SONG: "Yield Not to Temptation"

SILENT PRAYER (soloist sings softly the chorus): "Yield Not to Temptation"

TALK (by the superintendent): "Meeting a Serious Question"

Sooner or later most of you will be faced with the temptation to drink beverage alcohol—beer, wine, cocktails, or whiskey. When this time comes you will have to answer the questions as a Christian: What should I do about this matter of drinking? What should my attitude be? As Christians let us answer.

(NOTE.—Previously assign the following parts to sincere Christians. Ask that they be given without announcement. If preferred, all may sit at the front and proceed as a panel, the superintendent sitting with the group and guiding the discussion. Insist that no part be read.)

1. *I regard my body as a temple of the Holy Spirit.*—Since alcohol harms the body, especially, the brain and nervous system, it would be a sin for me to drink. Note what God's Word says: "Do you know that you are God's Sanctuary and that the Spirit of God dwells within you? If anyone destroys the Sanctuary of God, God will destroy him; for

220

the Sanctuary of God is sacred, and this sanctuary you are" (1 Cor. 3:16-17 Weymouth).

2. *Alcoholic indulgence results in inferior performance.*—I cannot afford as a Christian to give less than my best. Therefore, drinking is wrong for me. Dr. Walter Miles of Yale conducted extensive experiments on the effects of small amounts of alcohol on human efficiency. He found that even a small amount of alcohol, such as that found in an ordinary bottle of beer, retards all the body reflexes from 6 to 10 per cent for several hours.

3. *Since beverage alcohol is detrimental to personality, as a Christian I cannot afford to drink.*—I know from observation that the drinker often becomes silly and sometimes irresponsible. He is subnormal, and often says and does things he would not ordinarily say and do.

4. *I know that beverage alcohol leads to questionable companions and places: therefore, I must abstain.*—Taverns, juke joints, liquor stores, roadhouses, and the like are not fit places for a Christian youth. Drinking, swaggering young people are not fit companions for one who has been redeemed by the blood of Christ.

5. *My study of the liquor problem has revealed that alcohol is the accomplice of crime, the handmaiden of prostitution, the brother of gambling, and the friend of all other vices.*—Therefore, as a Chris-

tian I cannot drink. Sociologists tell us that liquor is the cause or ally of every vice practiced by men. Therefore, liquor must be scrupulously avoided by the Christian. "Come out from among them, and be ye separate, saith the Lord" (2 Cor. 6:17).

6. *Since alcohol is a habit-forming drug, I cannot afford to take the first drink.*—While many who drink do not become alcoholics, we know that "liquor's wrecks come exclusively from first drinkers," as Dr. John L. Hill reminds us. Dr. W. J. Mayo said that three of every ten drinkers become addicts, or slaves to liquor.

7. *I know that all money spent on beverage alcohol is wasted.*—Every dollar spent for liquor might go for something useful, such as groceries, fuel, clothing, or insurance. In 1945, Americans spent nearly eight billion dollars for alcoholic drinks, an average of $58 per capita. I have no money to waste on liquor.

8. *Since liquor destroys character, as a Christian I cannot afford to indulge in it.*—Federal Judge Patrick T. Stone, of Wisconsin, says: "From my experience on the bench, I have concluded that more boys and girls go bad because of drink than for any other reason. Drink quickly leads to all forms of dishonor." "Whether therefore ye eat, or drink, or whatsoever ye do, do all to the glory of God" (1 Cor. 10:31).

9. *Because liquor wrecks homes, I must be careful to avoid all alcoholic drinks.*—Dr. T. F. Adams says, "The home has no greater enemy than liquor in all its forms." Dr. Joy Elmer Morgan, famous educator says, "There is no question but that the increase in the use of both liquor and tobacco is doing vast and serious harm to school children by weakening their homes morally and economically."

10. *Since liquor is the enemy of the church and spiritual life, I must refrain from drinking.*—Liquor manufacturers are opposed to the church because the church attacks liquor. Alcohol obscures spiritual vision, blights spiritual growth, leads to the broad way and not to the straight and narrow path. Paul says, "Be not drunk with wine, wherein is excess; but be filled with the spirit" (Eph. 5:18).

CONCLUSION (by the superintendent): Suppose we list the objections to alcoholic beverages as just given on the blackboard. Does not alcohol, indeed, stand condemned? Surely, for these reasons we can see that drinking is incompatible with the Christian life; therefore we do not or will not drink and we shall use our influence to keep others from drinking.

SOLO: "Dare to Be Brave, Dare to Be True"

PRAYER

TOBACCO STANDS INDICTED

C. Aubrey Hearn

(NOTE.—Write to the National Education Association, 1201 Sixteenth Street, N. W., Washington, D. C., for a supply of the leaflet, "Shall I Become a Smoker?" by A. H. Steinhaus [one cent a copy for twenty-five or more]. See that each member of the department has a copy. Arrange a long table about which the members of the panel composed of the leader, several girls and boys, two teachers, and the pastor are seated. Display any material or statistics available on this subject on the table or walls.)

PRELUDE: "My Desire"

SONG (first stanza and chorus): "My Desire"

OPENING STATEMENT (by the superintendent): As you know, the use of tobacco is quite general in our country. For many years there has been a high-pressure advertising campaign by the tobacco companies to persuade people to smoke. The increase of smoking among women, and the emphasis upon smoking during the war, especially by the men in service, made cigarette consumption in the United States jump from 135 billion cigarettes in 1935 to 335 billion in 1945. (This was an average of 66 cigarettes per day for every person in the United States.)

The masses of the people are ignorant of the facts about tobacco. A dispassionate study of the tobacco problem leaves tobacco indicted upon six grounds.

QUARTET (first stanza and chorus unannounced): "Yield Not to Temptation"

PANEL DISCUSSION: On the blackboard write in large letters, Tobacco Stands Indicated, Because—and as the different reasons are brought out by the panel list them on the blackboard.

1. *Tobacco is a poison.*—Yes, indeed, tobacco does stand indicted because nicotine is defined right here in my dictionary by Webster as "A very poisonous alkaloid, the active principle of tobacco."

Dr. Kress in his book, *The Cigarette as a Physician Sees It,* says: "Nicotine is the poison depended upon by gardeners to kill insects and pests on plants. It is so deadly that it must be employed in a very dilute form, only a few drops to the pint of water. So virulent a poison is it that physicians have for years refrained from prescribing it. There is no antidote for tobacco poisoning."

There are eighteen other poisons in tobacco but nicotine is the most harmful. Dr. Steinhaus declares that 60 milligrams of nicotine injected into a man's blood would kill him. Of the 18 milligrams of nicotine injected into a cigarette only about two are absorbed by the lungs in smoking. A cigar equals five cigarettes.

Surely this suffices to show that the smoker inhales poison and thus indicts tobacco.

2. *Tobacco is a menace to health.*—A young man once asked Dr. Oliver Wendell Holmes a series of

questions as to what he would advise a young man to do. One of his questions was, Shall he smoke? Dr. Holmes answered: "Certainly not. It is liable to injure the sight, to render the nerves unsteady, to enfeeble the will, and enslave the nature to an imperious habit likely to stand in the way of duty to be performed."

Dr. John H. Kellogg in his book *Tobaccoism* describes how tobacco injures health.

Another doctor says: "I am going to explain, as well as I can in a few words, why the cigarette is bad for you. Cigarette smoking is bad because it strikes at the very root of life—the breathing.

"When you smoke a cigarette or breathe the air of a smoky room, the smoke enters directly into the lungs—and settles on the delicate membrane covering the surface of the lungs. This deposit clogs up the surface of the lungs and prevents both the escape of poison from the blood and the entrance of the oxygen of the air into the blood."

3. *Tobacco is habit-forming.*—Many people who use tobacco will tell you that it is bad but that they can't stop. There are few bad habits harder to break than smoking. In the *Reader's Digest* for July, 1940, there is an article by Courtney Ryley Cooper entitled "I Quit Smoking," which will give you some idea how difficult it is to stop smoking. Mr. Cooper

conquered the tobacco habit, however, and he testifies: "There exists no doubt about the benefits derived from cutting out tobacco. Of my friends who have stopped nibbling nicotine, all but two or three are feeling more fit. . . . Smoker's throat and cough has disappeared."

Smoking is filthy.—Smoker's breath and smoker's fingers are evidences of a filthy habit. This smell is offensive to some people of refined tastes. Those who have to live with tobacco users will testify that ash trays, smoking stands, smoke-filled rooms, and tobaccoish clothes are all tokens of the filth which accompanies the use of tobacco.

Smoking is wasteful.—America spent more than three billion dollars in 1944 for tobacco. This was more than was spent for all religious causes. This money goes up in smoke. There is nothing to show for it. Smokers justify the expense on the grounds of personal pleasure derived from the use of tobacco, and yet many of them admit that they would be better off without it.

Smoking is dangerous.—It is not uncommon to read about fires caused by smoking. "Some fires have their origin through a smoker falling asleep in bed while smoking. In a certain university a memorial hall, built after years of sacrifice on the part of pioneers, was destroyed in a few hours by a fire attributed to a freshman's cigarette. Cigarettes have been responsible for not a few forest fires. It is estimated that approximately one-third of all fires are due to the carelessness of smokers."

CONCLUSION (by the superintendent): There are many other indictments which can be made against tobacco but surely these six (review from blackboard) are sufficient to prove that tobacco is detrimental to all-round Christian growth. Definitely each of you can say of tobacco what was said of Belshazzar, "Thou art weighed in the balances, and are found wanting."

Will you, if this habit is yours, determine this morning for your own sake and for Jesus' sake to give it up?

QUARTET (chorus only): "Yield Not to Temptation"

PRAYER

228

PROMOTION DAY PROGRAM

Mrs. Frank S. Woodruff

INSTRUMENTAL SOLO: "He Leadeth Me"

PLAYLET: "The Journey of Life"

(NOTE.—All the parts are to be taken by members of the graduating classes. Ask them to assemble in one of the classrooms and each to come out when time to appear on the program. The Traveler carries a traveling bag. As each of the thirteen appears place a placard at the front of the department on which is printed the name of the thing packed which he represents. If preferred the program may be written on folders cut in the form of traveling bags.)

The Traveler: The time has come for me to leave our Intermediate department. On this journey into the unexplored future I shall be required to depend more upon myself and upon the training I have received in the past.

As I packed my grip for this trip, I was very careful to take only the things that would be most useful to me. I do not wish to be burdened with things which will slow me down in my journey or perhaps cause me to stumble and fall. As I show you what I have chosen to take with me, you may be the judge as to whether or not I have made a wise selection. Here I shall show you my possessions.

Prayer (pianist plays softly, "Sweet Hour of Prayer"): I am Prayer. My Intermediate friend is taking me with her because the Bible teaches each of us to "watch and pray, that ye enter not into temptation." "The effectual fervent prayer of a righteous man availeth much" (James 5:16).

Faith (pianist plays softly, "Faith Is the Victory"): I am Faith. Without faith in Christ my friend would often become discouraged and tempted to end the journey. "Now faith is the substance of things hoped for, the evidence of things not seen" (Heb. 11:1). "Therefore being justified by faith, we have peace with God through our Lord Jesus Christ" (Rom. 5:1).

Character (pianist plays softly, "Whiter Than Snow"): I am Character. Without me my friend's journey would end in misery and dishonor. In Proverbs 22:1 we read, "A good name is rather to be chosen than great riches, and loving favour than silver and gold."

Golden Rule (pianist plays softly, "Somebody"): I am Golden Rule. How often I am thoughtlessly cast aside! "Therefore all things whatsoever ye would that men should do to you, do ye even so to them."

Love (pianist plays softly, "Love Is the Theme"): I am Love. My friend, I hope you will guard me carefully that I may never become tarnished. In 1 John 4:7-8 we find "Beloved, let us love one another: for love is of God; and everyone that loveth is born of God, and knoweth God. He that loveth not knoweth not God; for God is love."

Forgiveness (pianist plays softly, "Into My Heart"): I am Forgiveness. My mission is to relieve the heartaches caused by thoughtlessness. "For if ye forgive men their trespasses, your heavenly Father will also forgive you" (Matt. 6:14).

Happiness (pianist plays softly, "I Am Satisfied with Jesus"): I am Happiness. Being a Christian, my friend was unwilling to travel without me. Christians are the happiest people on earth. The Bible teaches that, "Happy is he that hath the God of Jacob for his help, whose hope is in the Lord his God" (Psalm 146:5).

Honesty (pianist plays softly, "My Desire"): I am Honesty. My friend realizes that without me her journey would end in trouble and disgrace. In Acts 24:16 we read, "Herein do I exercise myself, to have always a conscience void of offence toward God, and toward men."

Kindness (pianist plays softly, "Help Somebody Today"): I am Kindness. I exert a great influence in life, and form many lasting friendships. In Ephesians 4:32 the apostle says, "Be ye kind one to another, tenderhearted, forgiving one another, even as God for Christ's sake hath forgiven you."

Knowledge (pianist plays softly "I Know the Bible Is True"): I am Knowledge. My friend has chosen wisely as the value of knowledge resulting from education is inestimable. In Proverbs 1:7 we

231

read, "The fear of the Lord is the beginning of knowledge."

Purity (pianist plays softly "I Need Thee Every Hour"): I am Purity. My friend's journey will not be clouded with regrets while I am with her. "Blessed are the pure in heart: for they shall see God" (Matt. 5:8).

Patience (pianist plays softly "Footsteps of Jesus"): I am Patience and many there are who neglect to take me on the journey of life. When affairs become burdensome I am often cast aside. Let us remember the words spoken in Hebrews 12:1, "Wherefore seeing we also are compassed about with so great a cloud of witnesses, let us lay aside every weight, and the sin which doth so easily beset us, and let us run with patience the race that is set before us."

Temperance (pianist plays softly "Yield Not to Temptation"): I am Temperance. Many fine characters are blighted by intemperance. In Ephesians 5:18 we read, "And be not drunk with wine, wherein is excess, but be filled with the spirit."

The Traveler: All these possessions are most valuable and necessary to a successful journey. As I leave the Intermediate department and proceed to a new experience it is my prayer that I along with my fellow graduates shall use these possessions daily and that each of us may become an inspiration to other travelers.

SOLO: "Make Me a Channel of Blessing"

AWARDING DIPLOMAS: by the superintendent

GRADUATING CLASS SUMMONED (superintendent of the Young People's department comes for them)

DEPARTMENT BLESSING (quoted by the entire department): Numbers 6:24-26

SONG (sung as the graduating classes pass to the Young People's department): "Take the Name of Jesus with You"

WELCOME TO NEW INTERMEDIATES: by superintendent

CLASS-TO-CLASS PROMOTION

PRAYER

FOLLOWING ON
(Promotion Day)

Mrs. C. H. Cosby

Plans.—Have a meeting of the graduating classes at least two weeks before Promotion Day and talk over the plans for the program. Assign parts to those best suited according to their ability and willingness to enter into the spirit of the occasion.

Materials Needed.—The department secretary should see that the following materials are placed in every classroom not later than Saturday afternoon, so that everything will be in readiness on Sunday morning: Classification slips (two for each pupil), teacher's record book, pencils, pupil's lesson quarterlies (the teacher's quarterly should have been given out the previous Sunday).

See that every one understands the plans so that no one will be ill at ease. No announcements should be necessary as the service moves forward. If possible, have the program mimeographed and give each person a copy.

Decorations.—Appoint a committee from the third-year classes to make the department attractive. Ferns and flowers must be used. Avoid elaborate or fussy decorations. Arrange chairs for graduates across front of room (facing audience), with a table and chair for the superintendent at one side. Tie the diplomas with department colors and place them on table, either in a basket or stacked between book ends.

(Note.—Give each person a record envelope and a pencil as he enters and ask that these be kept until the report is called for.)

Ushers.—Representatives from the third-year boys' class may serve as ushers.

PROGRAM

(Note.—At the first notes of the processional all stand while the graduates led by ushers and followed by the superintendent and teachers come down the aisle to their places.)

Piano and Violin Meditation: "Wherever He Leads I'll Go"

Processional: "He Leadeth Me"

Prayer

Records: Reports are filled as superintendent calls the six points. Ushers pass plates and collect reports and pencils while music is played.

Duet: "Footsteps of Jesus"

A Backward Glance (by president of girls' graduating class): Four years ago we of the graduating class came into this assembly room with a desire to be the best group ever to go through the Intermediate department. We admit we felt a bit strange and somewhat bewildered when we came but the fine welcome we received and the hearty way in which everyone seemed to enter into the work soon put us at our ease.

Many changes have come but in looking back over our four years in this department we find that: (Give a brief history of your class during the four years, giving it a spiritual rather than a material emphasis.)

During these four years we learned that we had to put in our very best if we would match the work of the other classes. We found plenty of competition, our notion to "outdo" gave place to a purpose to "do well."

HERE AND NOW (by president of boys' class): Our hearts are sad today because we love this place and all that it stands for. We know we have friends here, a superintendent who believes in us, teachers who understand us, and a host of friends among the younger classes. It's great to be a graduate!

As we go we become "freshies" again. We are going to have to find our places in the Young People's department as we did here four years ago.

While we are sad because we are leaving the Intermediate department we are also glad because of what these years have brought into our lives. Glad for the assurance we have that God is real and that Jesus is our Saviour and friend. Glad for the confidence we have in the Bible as God's Word and for the great truths we have hidden in our hearts. Glad for the privilege of going on as organized Sunday school classes doing the practical, worth-while things in our Christian service. Yes, we are glad that today is ours.

SOLO: "Thy Word Have I Hid in My Heart"

STRAIGHT AHEAD (by a girl): We hear our Captain's call, we will not hesitate, there is much more ahead. We read in 1 Corinthians 8:2, "If any man think that he knoweth anything, he knoweth nothing yet as he ought to know." So we move on and turn over to you third-year classes all our senior dignity along with our classrooms and all there is in them, including our most excellent teacher. To you we say "Be worthy."

We came into the department wanting to learn to do well—we go out wanting to translate that purpose into deeds as we struggle "for the prize of the high calling of God in Christ Jesus."

A PULL FROM ABOVE (by the superintendent): As your superintendent, I want to say that we are proud of you young people and as you go out of our department this morning you are not going out of our hearts. We will always be interested in you and eager to hear of your experiences.

God has given each of you a will and you must choose the road you wish to travel. To will to do God's will gives victory. Never feel sorry for yourself. Be a leader of the best and not a follower of weak, indifferent people. Take hold and work with God. He is trying to get certain things done. Do find out what these things are. Then get into line and help. Make the world more beautiful as you go through life. I do not know what life holds for you but I do know that God will never let go of you. No matter where you go you can never get away from his love. You may wander far but there will always be that tugging in your heart which will bring you back into his way. Take this verse, mark it in your Bible, hold it in your heart, Psalm 71:16, "I will go in the strength of the Lord God." Attempt great things, success is yours. Turn neither to the right nor to the left but follow on. He is leading. Always ask God to lead you and life will be one glad song of victory.

Will you stand? As I give you these diplomas I want to assure you again of our confidence in you to make good. We love you and we glory in your fine Christian strength.

SPECIAL RECOGNITION (by superintendent): Recognize individuals and classes that have won special honors during the year.

(NOTE.—Representatives from Young People's department [young man and lady] come to take graduating classes to Young People's department.)

PRAYER (by superintendent, all standing)

RECESSIONAL (All stand as graduating classes march out. Pianist continues playing as the ushers lead the new classes from the Junior department to the seats just vacated by the sixteen-year classes): "Lead On, O King Eternal"

238

SONG (all remain standing): "Just As I Am, Thine Own to Be"

Tune: "Just As I Am"

Just as I am, Thine own to be,
Friend of the young, who lovest me,
To consecrate myself to Thee,
O Jesus Christ, I come, I come.

.   .   .   .

Just as I am, young, strong, and free,
To be the best that I can be
For truth, and righteousness and Thee,
Lord of my life, I come, I come.

—MARIANNE HEARN. From *The Broadman Hymnal.*

WE WELCOME YOU (by superintendent. Word of welcome to the new pupils.)

SCRIPTURE READING (by department): Psalm 100

INTRODUCTION OF TEACHERS TO CLASSES

CLASS TO CLASS PROMOTION

ANNOUNCEMENTS: There will be only a brief period in the classrooms where teachers will get acquainted with pupils, classification slips are filled in, quarterlies and assignments are given out.

PRAYER

UNTO THE LEAST OF THESE
(Orphanage Program)

Mary Alice Biby

CHORUS: "There Shall Be Showers of Blessings"

MEDITATION (led by superintendent as duet sings, "Count Your Blessings")

(NOTE.—Print across the front of the blackboard, Blessings for which I am grateful. As duet sings let different boys and girls pass to the blackboard and list one blessing. Follow this with a season of quiet meditation as with bowed heads all meditate upon the cost of these blessings. While heads remain bowed have the first stanza of "I Gave My Life for Thee" sung softly by a concealed duet.)

SENTENCE PRAYERS (thanking God for blessings received)

SCRIPTURE READING (by a good reader): Matthew 25:32-46

DISCUSSION (led by superintendent): Suppose we think of the least of these this morning. I note that some of you listed the blessing of home on the blackboard. There are thousands of boys and girls your age who do not have a home or even parents to care for them.

The Baptists of our state have endeavored to make a home at (city) for (number) of these "little ones." It is known as our State Baptist Orphanage. (Name) is the superintendent. I have asked (name of girl) to tell of the provision made for girls in this home and of their activities. (Name of boy) will tell of the provision made for the boys and their activities.

ILLUSTRATION (by superintendent):

A simple-hearted old shoemaker was sitting in his shoeshop—his only home. One night he laid down to sleep, and in his sleep he dreamed that Jesus came and said, "I will take breakfast with you in the morning." Simple-hearted and faithful he arose the next morning to prepare breakfast for his royal guest. He spread his table with the cleanest cloth, and fried his ham with a delicate hand, and made his biscuits the very finest he could prepare, and then walked up the steps to look for Jesus, but he didn't come.

A little child came along crying. She had no hat upon her head, and the shoemaker said to her, "Child, what are you crying about?" She said, "I have nothing to eat; I slept under the steps last night; I have no home to go to." And he said to her, "Come with me; I have something for you to eat."

They sat down at his table, and he divided his breakfast with the little child.

The next night he laid down to sleep, and as he laid upon his bed he dreamed that Jesus came to his bed again. He said, "Why, Jesus, you disappointed me this morning; you said you were coming to take breakfast with me but you did not come." Jesus said, "I took breakfast with you in the person of that little child. 'Inasmuch as you have done it unto the least of these, ye have done it unto me.'"

—Taken from *Service*, compiled by Euclid B. Rogers, D.D., published by The Springfield Library Publishing Company.

DUET (third stanza sung by concealed duet): "I Gave My Life for Thee"

CONCLUSION (by the superintendent): Since we have so many blessings and since Christ has done so much for us, I wonder how we, like the old shoe-maker, can do something for these little ones in our orphanage.

(NOTE.—The department may make plans for some contribution to the orphanage. It may be money to be given through the church, scrapbooks for the small children, a box of assorted goodies, or some homemade candy. Perhaps you would rather appoint someone to write to the orphanage and find out just what service your department can render.)

PRAYER

THANKSGIVING

Mrs. L. L. Chastain

(NOTE.—Stalks of corn, pumpkins, an appropriate picture and fruits [the last to be taken to a needy family] may be placed about the front of the department.)

CALL TO WORSHIP: "Help Somebody Today"

SONG: "Doxology"

COMMENTS (by the superintendent): "Why Praise God?"

(NOTE.—Write the following references on attractive assignment cards and distribute before the program: Psalm 75:1; Psalm 105:1-5; Psalm 103:1-5. After these have been read ask the entire department to read Psalm 100.)

SENTENCE PRAYERS: thanksgiving for God's many blessings

TESTIMONIES (voluntary): "One Thing for Which I Am Thankful"

(NOTE.—As these are given, they may be listed on the blackboard. Call for Scripture references, showing that each of the things mentioned is a gift from God. The following are a few suggestions:

Food: Psalm 136:1, 25

Clothes: Matthew 6:30

Church: Psalm 112:1

School: Proverbs 12:1b

Health: Psalm 30:2

Peace: John 14:27

Wealth: Deuteronomy 8:18

243

If there are things named for which no Bible verse can be given, they may be summed up in the verse, James 1:17.)

DISCUSSION (by the superintendent): We are commanded again and again in the Bible, and especially in the psalms, to give thanks unto God, to sing praises unto his name. We become so accustomed to the many blessings that are ours from day to day, that we take them for granted, and often fail to express our thanks to the Giver of all good and perfect gifts. Our hearts should be so filled with gratitude that no opportunity will be missed to express our thanks and appreciation. Suppose we list some ways of saying thank you on the blackboard. (Have boys and girls suggest things that they will do during the Thanksgiving season.) I am sure in doing these things each of you will make Thanksgiving mean much to others and so mean much to you.

POEM:

Strange how Thanksgiving means so much to
    me
This year! And yet perhaps not strange, be-
    cause
I stole an hour from out the day to pause
And estimate my blessings prayerfully.
I'd been subtracting only woes before,
Where on life's slate were many joys to add
And when I tallied these, I found I had
A total startling precious in its score.

Ah, how insidious, self pity! Poor?
I, with a roof of shelter, food, and health?
A father, mother, friends—in them a sure
Trust fund of love? And all of beauty's wealth?
So now I go about my work on wings,
While "Thank you, thank you, thank you" my
    heart sings.

—Adapted from "A Woman Counts
Her Blessings" (by Ethel Romig
Fuller), *Good Housekeeping*, No-
vember, 1938. Used by permission
of *Good Housekeeping*.

SONG: "Count Your Blessings"

A PARABLE (by the superintendent):

The Lord called two girls unto him and gave into
their keeping richest blessings. Unto one girl he gave
youth, and to the other he gave a loving heart. "These
blessings," said the Lord, "are to be guarded well. Use
them for me and they will bring you rich returns." And
straightway the Lord departed.

"So youth is all I get!" the first girl said with arro-
gance; "youth is no rich blessing. It is a common thing.
All girls have youth. I wanted beauty, wealth, and
power; popularity and a host of friends. Youth is no
blessing to be guarded well or used. I'll fling mine to the
winds of reckless pleasure." And so she did.

The second girl took up with grateful outstretched
hands the blessing she had received.

"A loving heart," she mused with thoughtful mien.
I'll use it loving people—rich, poor, old, young; all those
who are in need of love. I'll give my love away unstint-

ingly, like perfume from a flower. My winged heart shall carry it afar."

The Lord returned and called the two girls to him. "I gave you rich blessings," said the Lord. "What have you done with them?"

"I flung my youth away," the first girl said, and sighed. " 'Tis gone. I know not where. Pleasure was all I sought and it has fled."

"Ah, foolish girl! But what of you?" he asked the second girl.

She lifted shining eyes to him. She said, "If I should withhold love from any living thing, then I should perish. It flows as from a fountain never dry. The more I give, the more I have to give. It is as if I were an instrument of loving, held in thy mighty hands, O Lord!"

"Well done, my faithful daughter. You have used your blessing wisely and by sharing it, a rich return is yours. Behold! Beauty, power, a host of friends follow like a trail of light your loving heart."

—EDNA EWING KELLEY. Used by permission.

SONG: "I Surrender All"

CLOSING COMMENT (by the superintendent): Surely our greatest spiritual blessing is Jesus who has taught us that real joy is to share. Share! This is God's word, not man's, to his church, to you and to me. Share the good news of forgiveness and life with those for whom Christ died. Christ said to us, "Go ye into all the world, and preach the gospel to every creature." The blessings of salvation are doubly ours when we share them with our fellow men, for they then become blessings that bless. Shall we not remember and follow these suggestions in our daily living?

SONG: "Give of Your Best to the Master"

PRAYER

CHRISTMAS IN SCRIPTURE AND SONG

Mrs. E. A. Patterson

(NOTE.—This program will be more effective if given without the announcement of parts. Printed programs may be given out. A pyramid on which the girls are to stand may be made by stacking boxes in pyramid form and covering them with sheets of white crepe paper. There should be space for five girls on the first row, four on the second, three on the third, two on the fourth, and one on the fifth or top row. Where there is no platform or curtain, it will be very effective to have the girls enter and take their places on the pyramid while a hymn is being sung. Each girl wears a white costume and holds a lighted red candle in left hand. If the Scripture has not been memorized, the Bible may be held in right hand. The girl in the center of the base of the pyramid repeats Mary's prayer while kneeling; the others remain silent. All lights should be out, leaving the room dark except for the light of the candles.)

PRELUDE: "O Come, All Ye Faithful"

SCRIPTURE READING (by the fifteen girls standing on the pyramid): Matthew 2:1-11.

PRAYER

TRIO (by three boys): "We Three Kings of Orient Are"

SCRIPTURE READING (read by the girls on the pyramid): Luke 2:8

SOLO (by a pupil if possible): "While Shepherds Watched Their Flocks"

SCRIPTURE READING (read by the girls on the pyramid): Luke 2:9-14

SONG (two stanzas by department): "Hark, the Herald Angels Sing"

SCRIPTURE READING (read by the girls on the pyramid): Luke 2:15-19

SONG (two stanzas by the department): "Away in a Manger"

PRAYER

SCRIPTURE READING (read by girl at the base of the pyramid as she kneels): Luke 1:46-53

RESPONSE (by the department): "Silent Night, Holy Night"

SPIRIT OF CHRISTMAS

PLAYLET

Edna Ewing Kelley

CHARACTERS

SPIRIT OF CHRISTMAS: *An attractive sixteen-year girl dressed in a long, white dress or robe, wearing a crown wth a silver star on the front of it*

TWO FOURTEEN-YEAR GIRLS: *Carrying toys*

THREE INTERMEDIATE BOYS: *Two carry baskets of groceries and one carries the silver offering*

A SMALL INTERMEDIATE GIRL: *Wearing scanty, ragged clothing*

SCENE

Arrange the front of the assembly room as attractively as possible. Cedar and pine trees or branches sprayed with water and then sprinkled with flour will add to the effectiveness of the program.

(NOTE.—The three gifts presented by the Intermediate boys and girls [food, money, and toys] may be changed to meet local needs.)

SOFT MUSIC: A medley of Christmas songs

(NOTE.—Ask several who sing well to group themselves in different classrooms, singing a number of Christmas songs before the program begins.)

SONG (First stanza sung by all the groups as they come from the classrooms to their places in the assembly room): "Joy to the World"

250

SCRIPTURE READING (by one who reads well as department follow in their Bibles): Luke 2:8-16

PRAYER

SPIRIT OF CHRISTMAS (*enters*): I am the Spirit of Christmas. I have been in the world more than nineteen hundred years, representing the love of God, which gave the Christ Child to the world. I bring peace and good will to men. I scatter happiness and cheer wherever I go, making glad the hearts of all and filling them with the love of Christ each Christmas season.

(*Enter two boys carrying large baskets filled with groceries.*)

FIRST BOY: Spirit of Christmas, the boys in our class are bringing groceries for the Christmas dinner of a needy family. (*Sets basket on the floor at her feet*)

SPIRIT OF CHRISTMAS (*surprised*): But why are you boys who have all that you need interested in providing a Christmas dinner for someone less fortunate than yourselves?

SECOND BOY: Because, O Spirit of Christmas, you have entered our hearts and filled them with love for others. It is you who have given us a desire to help the needy this Christmas season.

SPIRIT OF CHRISTMAS: Through helping others, you serve the Lord. Christ himself said, "I was an hungred, and ye gave me meat" (Matt. 25:35).

(*Exit boys. Enter two girls with arms full of toys.*)

FIRST GIRL: Spirit of Christmas, the girls in our class are bringing toys for the children at the —— Orphans' Home.

SPIRIT OF CHRISTMAS: But why are you girls, who have so much pleasure in your lives, interested in bringing gifts that will make little children happy?

SECOND GIRL: Because, O Spirit of Christmas, you have entered our hearts and have filled them with the same love for little children which Jesus had. You have given us a desire to make them happy.

SPIRIT OF CHRISTMAS: Again our Lord said, "Inasmuch as ye have done it unto one of the least of these my brethren, ye have done it unto me" (Matt. 25:40).

(*Girls place toys at feet of Spirit of Christmas and then exit. Enter boy carrying bag of money.*)

BOY: Spirit of Christmas, I present to you an offering from the Intermediate department. It is a love gift of money to the missionaries who are carrying the gospel of Christ to the uttermost parts of the earth.

(NOTE.—If the church as a whole has a White Christmas program, Spirit of Christmas should turn the offering in at that time; if not, she may hand it to the church treasurer after Sunday school, or drop it in the offering plate at the preaching service.)

SPIRIT OF CHRISTMAS: But why are you young people who already know the blessings of the gospel interested in sending it to others?

BOY: Because, O Spirit of Christmas, you have entered our hearts, filling them with love that extends to every lost soul in all the world.

SPIRIT OF CHRISTMAS: You are indeed following Christ's commands for he said, "Go ye into all the world, and preach the gospel to every creature" (Mark 16:15).

(*Boy exits. Enter small girl, poorly clad, who holds out empty hands timidly, appealingly.*)

GIRL: O Spirit of Christmas, I have no gifts to bring for others; no food; no toys for little children; no gold that is mine to give. I have nothing to lay at your feet at this Christmas season.

SPIRIT OF CHRISTMAS: What! You have nothing to give, my child? You, with your heart of gold, have no rich gift to offer!

GIRL: My heart is a small gift, O Spirit of Christmas. I would humbly, gladly lay it at the feet of the Christ Child, but it seems so little in return for all of the love which Christ has given me.

SPIRIT OF CHRISTMAS: But Christ said to you, "Give me thine heart" (Prov. 23:26).

253

GIRL: Then in loving service I now present to him my heart, my life—my all. (*Kneels in front of Spirit of Christmas.*)

SOLO (sung by girl): "All, Yes All, I Give to Jesus"

SPIRIT OF CHRISTMAS: On the birthday of our Lord the shepherds brought their praise and the wise men brought their riches; the young people brought their love gifts, but you, "O daughter of Zion," having nothing to bring, offer the greatest gift of all—yourself. May each member of the department think earnestly on this matter and being led by the Holy Spirit "give your all to Christ"—the greatest Christmas present. (*Spirit of Christmas lifts arms in signal for department to rise. All sing last stanza of "Joy to the World."*)

PRAYER

MISCELLANEOUS

SERVE THE LORD WITH GLADNESS

(Department Scheme)

Mrs. J. L. McCutcheon

(NOTE.—Display an attractive poster giving the department scheme as follows: Name, Intermediate Department; Colors, gold and dark blue; Aim, To Serve the Lord with Gladness; Scripture, Psalm 100; Song, "Serve the Lord with Gladness.")

PRELUDE: "Serve the Lord with Gladness"

SONG (first stanza): "Serve the Lord with Gladness"

SCRIPTURE READING (read by the department): Psalm 100

SENTENCE PRAYERS

DISCUSSION (by the superintendent): I have placed our department scheme at the front of the department. Suppose we all read our aim. What are some ways we may carry out this aim? (Voluntary response. See that the following are brought out: Attend the church services, visit the sick, help the poor, and the like.)

But how about washing dishes, mowing the lawn, mending clothes, running errands, and all the homely everyday tasks that most of us must do? Can we possibly think of these as services to God and do them gladly?

SONG (first and second stanzas): "Building, Daily Building"

QUESTION (by the superintendent): Does it not all depend on the spirit in which the work is done, whether grudgingly or willingly, cheerfully or resentfully, with gladness as stated in our aim or slightingly, reluctantly? Just how do you feel about your service? What can you do to improve it? What will you do?

SCRIPTURE MEDITATION (led by superintendent as all open Bibles to Psalm 100): We have discussed the opening admonition but have you counted your blessings that you may come before him with thanksgiving? Have you thought a great deal of his mercy?

SOLO (second and third stanzas): "Serve the Lord with Gladness"

SONG STUDY (led by the superintendent): Now let us study the message in our department song. As you name the things suggested for daily conduct as found in our song I shall write them on the blackboard.

As we think of our aim, Bible verse, and song, I trust each of you will endeavor to put these thoughts into your daily conduct. Why not check each night to see if you have really lived our department scheme during the day. (Give each of them a copy.)

STORY (by the superintendent): He was injured at birth. Every word he has spoken throughout his life has been spoken with difficulty; every step made with greatest effort; every movement of the arms, or hands, has called for real labor. Often every bite eaten is fed him by a loving mother or father. And yet, to come into his presence is to have one's soul stirred to its innermost depths.

His faith is supreme; his prayer life most beautiful. The stammering tongue tells others of the Christ who could make a cripple boy overcome physical handicaps in the joy of spiritual wholeness. His tongue daily testifies for Jesus and ever speaks the encouraging, joyful, optimistic word for him.

Those trembling unbalanced limbs are made, through sheer will power, guided by the Holy Spirit, to carry him to the church he loves, on missions of mercy, and to places of usefulness. He has wrought for good where others have failed. He has turned physical disappointments into "his appointments." Truly throughout his life he has been a living example of one who serves the Lord "with gladness."

POEM: "Yielded for Service"

I come to thee to bring my mind,
  Wide open to thy word 'tis brought;
O fill it with thy truth divine,
  And help me think thy lovely thought.

I come to thee to bring this heart
  Of mine, that it may loving be;
O love divine, thy warmth impart
  To it, that I may feel with thee.

I come to thee to bring my will,
  I yield it now to thee alone;
O make it thine—thy plan fulfil—
  To choose with thee before thy throne.

I go with thee to work today,
  Our minds, our hearts, our wills make one
In worship sweet, to serve thy way,
  Our work to do until it's done.

> —ELBERT N. JOHNSON, in *The Teacher*.
> Used by permission.

CHORUS: "Serve the Lord with Gladness"

PRAYER

THE STANDARD OF EXCELLENCE

Mrs. W. W. West

(NOTE.—Pamphlets on reaching and maintaining the class and department Standards may be tacked about the assembly room to give atmosphere. Carry out the Intermediate color scheme [blue and gold], with yellow flowers in blue vases. Before the opening period, hang a large piece of white poster board, or wrapping paper on the blackboard or wall, on which to place the cutout parts of the Standard of Excellence which have been previously assigned to the associate superintendent and five pupils.)

SCRIPTURE READING: "Lift Up a Standard"— Isaiah 59:19*b*

INSTRUMENTAL DUET (piano and violin): "Onward Christian Soldiers"

SONG: Onward Christian Soldiers"

TALK (by the superintendent): "Starting a New Sunday School Year"

This is the beginning of a new Sunday school year. You boys and girls have new teachers and of course you teachers have new pupils. We are starting again with new record cards. This should inspire us to make some new resolutions and to plan for our work. That reminds us of our department guide. All important organizations have well-planned procedures. Before a building is constructed plans are drawn and blueprints made from which to work. Suppose we ask our associate superintendent to read the reasons for having an Intermediate Sunday school department.

SOFT MUSIC: "Bring Them In"

(NOTE.—As this is played the associate superintendent comes to the front, reads the objective, which has been cut from the top of the Standard of Excellence, and fastens it to the top of the poster.)

DISCUSSION (by the superintendent, pointing to the objective): Reaching boys and girls is one of our most serious and difficult problems. We work to interest those that are not interested and to persuade the inactive class members to attend regularly. I wonder what class will show the greatest improvement in regular attendance. Suppose the girls challenge the boys to a better attendance record during the next three months.

We have some real help on this if we follow our guide, the Standard of Excellence—truly a guide for all class and department activities. It is a blueprint of our plans and a measuring rod for all Southern Baptist Intermediate Sunday school work—a worthwhile program. Suppose we see what these parts are.

(NOTE.—Ask those who have the other parts of the Standard chart to come to the front, read their requirements and fasten them to the poster.)

DISCUSSION (by the pianist): New Testament churches are evangelistic. Southern Baptists have always majored in evangelism. This explains our growth. Our fathers preached the gospel, called sinners to repentance, baptized, and indoctrinated the saved. So must we. (As my Father hath sent me even so send I you.)

RESOLUTION (by a man teacher)

(NOTE.—Ask this teacher to offer a resolution that the department adopt the Standard of Excellence as a guide. Have this voted on by the department.)

This Standard of Excellence which we have adopted today is offered for Intermediate departments and this one (show Standard) is offered for Intermediate classes. Please study your class Standard at your next class meeting. These Standards are simple, definite, and practical. If used, they will keep us from getting lopsided in our interests and from wasting time. They may serve to measure our progress and to show both the strong and weak points. They have distinctly spiritual emphasis.

RESOLUTION (by a teacher)

(NOTE.—Ask this teacher to offer a resolution that the department will endeavor to reach the Standard of Excellence in the next three months. Vote on this.)

PRESENTATION (by the song leader)

(NOTE.—The chorister presents the department with a beautifully mounted Standard of Excellence chart. Hang this over the poster which has just been completed.)

ACCEPTANCE AND COMMENTS (by the superintendent)

(NOTE.—Accept the poster with an expression of appreciation and put seals on the points already attained calling attention to the requirements for which the pupils are responsible.)

The Standard of Excellence is not an end but a means for reaching an end. It is an outline of things to be done. It is a challenge. What class will be the first to use each of the ten requirements?

SONG: "Our Best"

PRAYER: asking God's blessings on the department and help in keeping the resolutions made

RECORDS

Lizzie Waite

(NOTE.—Place a Six Point Record System chart on the wall. Have the letters RECORDS written on the blackboard and during talks fill in outline. Write the Scripture references on small Bibles cut from construction paper, and hand them out to pupils, before the program begins.

Records on high—Job 16:19; Every one shall give an account—Romans 14:12; Christ our foundation—1 Corinthians 3:11; Order—1 Corinthians 14:40; Rewards—Matthew 6:1; Diligence—Hebrews 6:11-12; Sincerity—Joshua 24:14a. Give every person present a Six Point Record slip and a pencil on arrival.)

CALL TO WORSHIP: "Higher Ground"

SONG (first stanza): "Higher Ground"

SCRIPTURE READING (by the department): Genesis 17:1b

DISCUSSION (led by the superintendent): "Marking Records"

As I call each point, will each of you mark your record simultaneously this morning and hold your envelope before you as we discuss it? You may take this envelope to your class and use it for your record. Sometimes we look upon our records as something the superintendent or the secretary or somebody else insists on, but we do not think it is very important. Unless we stop and check on ourselves we may fail to give it an important place in our worship service. But you say, how can marking myself on a slip of paper as being present, on time, and so forth, be a part of worship? Let us see if we can find anything in our record that may be called worship.

(Call for Job 16:19.) Where is my record? (Voluntary response.) Is this record I hold in my hand a part of my life record? (Voluntary response.) So this record is "on high." Does that give importance to your record this morning?

(Call for Romans 14:12.) What am I to give an account of ? (Voluntary response.) To whom am I to give this account? (Voluntary response.) To God! If I must give an account of myself, then I will have to give an account to God of how I mark this record this morning.

(Call for 1 Corinthians 3:11.) Do you think that means that my Sunday school record has Christ for its foundation? Yes, this record is a part of my life's record that is kept in heaven, and I must give an account of that record to God. Surely then the record I make in his house should be founded on Christ.

(Call for 1 Corinthians 14:10.) Have you ever seen records taken when it was not done decently and in order? As we mark our records let us remember that verse, "Let all things,"—even the taking of your individual record, "be done decently and in order."

(Call for Matthew 6:1.) Does this seem a strange verse to read in connection with records? What do

265

you think this verse means? (Voluntary response.)
Yes, Jesus is teaching that all acts of worship should
be of God. We are not to be like the hypocrites—to
be seen of men. Are you striving for a good record
to be seen of men, or to be seen of God? We are re-
warded either by men or by God. Which reward
are you working for? Of course, we like for others
to see our good records, we are proud of our name
on an honor roll, but is that all the reward you
want? A reward from God for our good record!
What a wonderful thought!

(Call for Hebrews 6:11-12.) What message do
we get from these verses? (Voluntary response.)
It seems then that we are not only to be careful
about the making of our record, but we are to see
that we have a good record. How diligent have you
been this week about your record for this morning?
You are here, but were you here on time? How
much time have you spent in the preparation of
your lesson? Were you ready with your Bible and
offering? Have you come prepared to stay throughout the entire morning service? Be diligent—not
slothful.

(Call for Joshua 24:14a.) How does Joshua say
we are to serve the Lord? (Voluntary response.)
It is not a trivial matter to put down on paper what
you have done for the Lord. Let us be sincere in
our worship.

SONG (first stanza): "Our Best"

CONCLUSION (by the superintendent): And now may I say one thing about your record. You are building character and every point on this record slip represents something you should have in your character if you are to fit yourself to give God your best service. That record slip you hold in your hand is really a picture of you. God wants us to use you in his service but he can only use the life you give him, the character you build. Electricity is a power we cannot understand. That power goes through the electric light bulb and makes light. That same electricity goes through iron and makes heat. That same electricity goes through other instrumentalities and makes power. It is the same electricity but what it accomplishes depends on what it has to go through. Just so, God's power can come into your life and into my life, but what that power accomplishes depends upon what kind of life we have prepared for it to go through. It is the same power that works in all of us, but we are not all furnishing the same kind of life for it to work through. Look at your record slip again. What can God's power accomplish through the life you are living, as shown by that record?

CHORUS: "Our Best"

PRAYER

OUR CHOICE

(Books)

Marie Estes Stopher

(Note.—Arrange a browsing table on which have been placed several books that fall under the different groups to be discussed. Be sure that these are books that appeal to Intermediates. Place attractive book jackets all about the department. Arrange a large Bible on the table at the center of the front of the assembly room.)

Soft Music: "Thy Word Have I Hid in My Heart"

Duet: "Wonderful Words of Life"

Prayer: of thanksgiving for the words of life and beauty stored up in great books

Scripture Reading (read by the department): 1 Kings 3:3-15

Discussion (by the superintendent): The story of Solomon's great choice is one that never fails to stir our admiration. It ought more to stir our shame, for whether we realize it or not, God offers to every boy and girl today the same choice. Immeasurable opportunities in the way of pleasures, personal triumphs, money accumulations, or wisdom. In the pursuit of wisdom, books cannot be neglected. There is an old proverb which reads,

Who without books essays to learn
Draws water in a leaky urn.

In other words, if you really want wisdom, it is utter foolishness to disregard the storehouse of wisdom's treasures: namely, books.

Your acceptance of the value of books involves cultivating good books, shunning the bad books, and letting the indifferent books alone.

Now the question comes: What is a good book? (Voluntary response.) Some may say, a good book is one that is easy to read, one that is exciting, thrilling, one that turns out all right, one that you want to read again, one that you think about after you've read it, one whose characters seem real. All of your answers, of course, point out certain elements of a good book, but the most valid test is whether the reading of the book inspires one consciously or unconsciously to be something finer and nobler than he was before.

In the process of time, certain well-defined types of reading and even particular titles have evolved as "best books." These books are made known to us in numbers of ways. How do we come to know about them? (Voluntary response.) Yes, our parents, teachers and friends tell us. We see them at the Baptist Book Store. The books are mentioned in our quarterlies at times. We have or need a church library that lends books and a librarian that makes us want to read them.

(If your church has a library call attention to its location in the church. Invite the librarian to be with you, and recognize her presence.)

We have drawn on the blackboard the outline of a bookshelf. (Make this the actual size of a bookshelf about ten inches tall.) Will each of you think of your own reading shelf? To get the most out of your reading what will you fill it with? Five of our Intermediates are going to give us suggestions. (Choose beforehand five Intermediates whom you know to be readers of good books. Provide them with pieces of construction paper cut to look like the back of a book. In other words, strips of varied height and width will give the effect. These strips should be lettered to indicate certain subject groupings—biography, fiction, hobby books, vocational books, history. Ask each pupil to come forward in turn, place his book back on the shelf, and make some statements concerning it.)

FIRST PUPIL: Each of us ought to fill part of his bookshelf with good biographical books. Biographies are not sissy books, they are even better than made-up stories. One biography I especially liked was (give name of book. If you have a copy on the browsing table show this.) I for one am going to keep on reading biography.

SECOND PUPIL: All of us like good fiction. We don't need much urging to read in this field, but we do need to be prodded about choosing the best there is. Recently I read (give name and show book). Not only was the story good, but the life principles of the main characters were inspiring.

Third Pupil: Hobby books are right up my alley. I like to make things and then, too, I like to collect things. Also, I am interested in seeing what others make and collect. The book (give name) surely gave me new ideas.

Fourth Pupil: I am still trying to decide on a vocation. Reading about the various opportunities and what people have done in these lines of work helps me.

Fifth Pupil: Some people don't like to read history, but history doesn't have to be dry and uninteresting. Humor, suspense, and action are all to be found in the best books on history. Besides, knowing what people have done before us helps us to form our plan of action. All of us ought to read history.

Conclusion (by the superintendent): If you will all follow a systematic plan of reading, habitually choosing good books, you will not only *know more* but will *be more*. Suppose you go to the church library and ask the librarian to help you select a book. Read it by next Sunday if possible, and come prepared to give at least one helpful result of reading the book. (Keep back of some of your boys and girls during the week so that a good report will come in. Endeavor to arouse interest in the accumulation of a personal library of helpful books.)

PRAYER

INSTALLATION PROGRAM

Mary Alice Biby

CALL TO WORSHIP: "Work, for the Night Is Coming"

PRAYER

INSTALLATION: by the superintendent

INTRODUCTORY COMMENTS (by the superintendent): "The Challenge of a Task"

SONG (first stanza as presidents stand): "To the Work"

(Give copies of the class Standard of Excellence to each with an impressive talk stressing the responsibility of leadership in their class. Explain the use of the Standard as a guide and urge each to endeavor to lead his class to attain the Standard.)

DUET (first stanza as the associate superintendent and vice-presidents stand): "Bring Them In"

(Give the associate superintendent a list of all absentees and prospects by classes. Give each vice-president a list of the absentees and prospects of his class. Challenge them to bring these in. Brief comments setting out the importance of reaching boys and girls.)

SOLO (as the secretary with the class secretaries stand): "Is My Name Written There?"

(Give the secretary the name of every member of the department. List pupils by classes. Place the grade for previous Sunday after the name of each pupil on this list. Give each class secretary the name of each pupil in his class with the grade for the previous Sunday. Comment by stressing opportunities for aiding in real character building. Urge each to improve his grade.)

QUARTET (as the song leader and chairman of activities stand): "Somebody"

(Give the chorister a calendar of suggestions for social activities asking that he work with the class chairman of activities in adjusting this to suit the needs of the department.

Give each chairman of activities a list of persons for whom service activities may be planned. Have pupils add to this list and to make suggestions of things to be done. Ask the chairman with the song leader to make out a practical calendar of activities to be carried out by the department.)

SONG (as pianist and chairman of stewardship and missions stand): "Send the Light"

(Give the pianist the names of all Christians in the department with a "T" after the names of all who tithe and also a "B" after the name of each who gives through the budget; urge those Christians not tithing or contributing, very tactfully, to do so.)

QUARTET (concealed voices): "Tell Me the Old, Old Story"

DUET (as teachers stand): "I Love to Tell the Story"

(Give each teacher a list of the unsaved in his class. Urge that he endeavor to win the unsaved to Christ and to inspire the saved to renewed consecration.)

INSTALLATION PRAYER

PLEDGE TO MY DEPARTMENT

Agnes Kennedy Holmes

SONG: "Higher Ground"

SCRIPTURE READING: Psalm 34:13-18

PRAYER: that each member may be loyal to class and to department.

(NOTE.—Typed or mimeographed copies of this program should be distributed. Ask questions alternately, first from the boys' pledge then from the girls'. Ask the boys and girls to read the last item in unison as it will be on both pledges alike. Let the men teachers pledge with the boys, and the women with the girls. After pledges have been given the leader should express gratification for their hearty co-operation and explain in a few words the significance of this pledge.)

BOYS PLEDGE: by leader and boys

Leader: When our department needs assistance what shall we do?

Boys: Call on us!

Leader: Suppose the church needs service that a boy can give?

Boys: We will help!

Leader: Who will try to be 100 per cent according to the Six Point Record System?

Boys: Trust us!

Leader: What is your pledge?

Boys: We shall strive to be loyal and faithful to our class, our department, to our church, and our God.

GIRLS PLEDGE: by leader and girls

Leader: When the department needs help that a girl can give what shall we do?

Girls: Try us!

Leader: Will any class endeavor to reach the Standard?

Girls: Depend on us!

Leader: How many will be present, on time, with Bibles brought from home, an offering, a prepared lesson, and remain for preaching?

Girls: We will!

Leader: What is your pledge?

Girls: We shall strive to be loyal and faithful to our class, our department, to our church, and our God.

Song: "Just As I Am, Thine Own To Be"

Prayer: for strength to keep this pledge